CONCILIUM

D0324992

concilium 1993/1

MESSIANISM THROUGH HISTORY

Edited by

Wim Beuken, Seán Freyne and
Anton Weiler

SCM Press · London
Orbis Books · Maryknoll, New York

Published by SCM Press Ltd, 26–30 Tottenham Road, London N1
and by Orbis Books, Maryknoll, NY 10545

February 1993

ISBN: 0334 03018 8 (UK)
ISBN: 0 88344 869 6 (USA)

Typeset at The Spartan Press Ltd, Lymington, Hants
Printed and bound in Great Britain by
Mackays at Chatham PLC, Chatham, Kent

Concilium: Published February, April, June, August, October, December

Contents

Editorial

The Messiah in History

I. Biblical

Just 250 years ago the first performance of Handel's oratorio, *Messiah*, took place in Dublin. This issue of *Concilium* is not, however, prompted by any nostalgic recollection of that rightly acclaimed cultural event, but has rather a more serious historical and theological rationale. In composing his great work Handel was able to draw on an earlier selection of texts from the Hebrew scriptures that purported to depict the Messiah's origins, career and destiny, with a peculiarly Christian bias. Yet a distinctly christological reading of those scriptures dates back to the first Christian century and was to form an important aspect of Christian apologetics for centuries. Consequently, belief in the figure of the Messiah, instead of providing a shared basis of hope for all who might seek to ground their religious faith in those Hebrew writings, became a stumbling block between Christians and Jews down to the present day.

A reconsideration of the idea of the Messiah is timely for a number of reasons. Biblical scholarship is becoming increasingly diversified in terms of the methodologies it employs, adding recent literary and social-scientific concerns to the more widely established historical approaches of the past. Accordingly, a rich diversity within those writings is emerging as varied social as well as historical contexts are seen to have given rise to more sharply focused portraits of received figures and images. Christian scholarship's claims to objectivity have rightly been questioned for its unilinear reading of the Hebrew scriptures and other Jewish writings, giving rise to the distinct impression of a clearly defined and univocal messianic hope in the first century, which then, it is claimed, was uniquely realized in the career of Jesus of Nazareth.

As long as the post-biblical Jewish writings were treated under the synthetic label 'rabbinic', there was little possibility of exploring the ways in which Jews continued to hope in the Messiah, despite the triumphant claims of Christianity, backed by the might of the Empire from the age of Constantine onwards. Neither was there likely to have been any great awareness of the importance of that belief for ongoing Jewish history in the mediaeval and modern periods in so far as Christian historians for the most part operated with the stereotype of a religion that was regarded as dessicated and drained of its capacity to revitalize its foundational stories to meet new exigencies of history.

Dialogue between Jews and Christians in the post-Auschwitz world, as well as the emergence of the scientific study of Judaism within academic circles, has helped to break down these stereotypes and bring to Jewish scholarship a new and self-confident agenda in terms of its own historical awareness and identity. Earlier in this century the studies of the great Jewish historian Gershom Scholem had opened up the topic of this number of *Concilium* in a highly significant way. More recently, other scholars have seen the need to speak about Messiahs in the plural in order to underline the fact that it is improper to think about *the* Messiah, as though only one account of the expectations engendered by that figure was either possible or legitimate.

It is important for Christians, scholars and lay people alike, to be more keenly aware of these biblical and historical developments, at a moment when Christian theology and praxis, especially in Third World situations, is beginning to rediscover and actively appropriate its own messianic self-understanding, based on the New Testament writings, especially the Gospels, as the article of Jon Sobrino shows. It is one of the ironies of the history of ideas that this Christian rediscovery of a messianic consciousness has been prompted more by dialogue with a secular version of these hopes mediated through Marxist thinking than through any great awareness of renewed Jewish theological or religious interest in the issue. As a matter of fact, the philosophical faith of Karl Marx contain some messianic elements, which are examined by Alistair Kee.

It is against the background of these discussions that this issue of *Concilium* was planned, and some, though not all, of these topics are explicitly dealt with in the pages that follow. It is impossible to cover every aspect of a complex topic in one issue of such a journal. Nevertheless, it is hoped that by laying solid foundations in biblical and historical reflections that are conscious of the contemporary issues, the way will be opened up for a more nuanced Christian understanding of the topic in the first instance, and new possibilities provided for more fruitful dialogue with our Jewish sisters and brothers in the future.

Not all accounts of a complex historical development can be expected to agree, especially when differing methodological approaches are adopted by scholars who address the issue with different concerns. Thus in the biblical section there is an inevitable overlapping as differing opinions surface about the origin and continued expression of belief in the Messiah within the biblical witness, depending on whether the author's focus is on the Hebrew scriptures (Beuken), extra-canonical Jewish writings (Horsley), or the New Testament (Freyne). These differences, especially between Beuken and Horsley, are based, partially at least, on the different perspectives of the authors – the former adopting a literary and the latter a sociological approach; the former concentrating on the world of text, the other on the world behind the text. For Beuken belief in the Messiah originated in the pre-exilic period, as can be seen in the treatment of the figure of 'Yahweh's anointed' in the Books of Samuel and the Psalms. This figure serves as an ideal against which the failings of the house of David are to be measured and becomes a cipher to express Israel's longing for complete redemption which it did not experience in and through the monarchy, thus enabling it to overcome the trauma of the exile. It is, therefore, a product of Israelite prophetic consciousness dating from the pre-exilic period, not an import of Near Eastern royal ideology as Horsley claims, by which the Davidic monarchy itself sought to legitimate its own position over against notions of what he calls 'popular kingship'.

Horsley's sociological approach, based on a theory of conflict, by which competing groups are seen to generate their own ideology of legitimation and liberation, finds ample evidence in the later biblical writings and other extra-canonical Jewish literature of the Second Temple period. In this regard the writings of the Jewish historian, Flavius Josephus, are particularly important in that from these one can glean echoes at least of alternative, popular movements to those represented by the scribal class who produced the bulk of the literature for upper classes. The survey of this diverse body of literature will surprise many who have been brought up to believe that expectation of the Messiah was the hallmark of Jewish faith in the period. In Horsley's account (as distinct from Beuken) the scattered references to the Messiah, even in Qumran, form no systematic or well-established pattern in terms of an expected Davidic end-time liberator. For him, the movements of popular kingship form the best analogue to the Jesus movement, whereas apocalyptic and other images of a transcendent figure are relevant to later Christian reflections about the special significance of Jesus.

Important as this challenging corrective is to the standard Christian account of Jewish expectations, it runs the risk of erring in the opposite direction. Certainly, the New Testament writings, especially the Gospels, point to a variety of expectations and speculations about the Messiah in contemporary Jewish circles. This is the point of departure of the article by Freyne, who seeks to allow these New Testament writings to speak to the issue in their own terms. There are undoubtedly different emphases in the formulation of Jesus' messianic role, which is nevertheless affirmed in all the writings. These differences can be explained in relation to the larger concerns of the writers, often in polemical contexts with competing Jewish groups, but also with reference to the social concerns of the various Christian groups being addressed. While agreeing with Horsley that we must avoid synthetic constructions of the Messiah that have more to do with Christian theology than actual, first-century, historical realities, Freyne would, nevertheless, see that the issue of the Messiah was more 'in the air' than one might suspect from a reading of Horsley's article. At the same time the variety of early Christian usage of the idea and the concern to integrate it with other images and symbols of liberation point to the probing, exploratory nature of early Christian confessions about Jesus' messianic status, rather than the absolute and definitive claims that have been made by Christian orthodoxy.

The issue of diversity of emphasis in different documents continues to be the concern of Jacob Neusner's pioneering work in the field of rabbinic scholarship. The absence of the Messiah in the foundation document of that corpus, the Mishnah, can be explained, partly at least, in terms of the political failures of the two 'messianic' wars against Rome (66–70 and 132–135 CE). The sages who framed the Mishnah were concerned to develop an alternative system for Israel, based on sanctification through order rather than salvation through militant, human action. The challenge to Israel is to fashion a life-style that would seek to ignore the vicissitudes of history. Yet memories of history, especially sorrowful ones, do not readily depart, so by the fourth century, Israel turned back to its history in order to learn the lessons of history in the Talmud of the land of Israel (Yerushalmi). Israel can never be autonomous; there is only a choice of master: God or the nations. Once that lesson of history has been learned, then the Messiah myth can return as part of Israel's history, as it does in this great collective work. However, the role of the Messiah is now utterly changed, in line with the fundamental philosophy framed by the Mishnah earlier – not as the agent of human achievement, but as the sage who will enable Israel to allow God to achieve God's will for Israel – sanctification rather than liberation.

The historical section is concerned to show how the messianic idea continued as a fruitful and challenging metaphor for Jews and Christians throughout history in different historical and cultural contexts. Many topics and figures were proposed to illustrate this diversity that continued to express itself in both Jewish and Christian circles, even when it might have been thought that for Christians the matter was already closed. The editors decided to focus on a few outstanding examples from both traditions rather than attempt a complete coverage. For Christian readers in particular it is salutary to discover the ways in which the Jewish tradition continued to engage the idea of the Messiah, particularly after it shed its political associations from the second century CE onwards in the rabbinic literature.

The issue of diversity of emphasis in different documents within the corpus of writings that was produced between the second and the fifth centuries CE is the major concern of Jacob Neusner's pioneering work in the academic study of Judaism. The absence of the Messiah in the foundation document of that collection, the Mishnah, can be explained in the light of the concerns of the sages to develop an alternative system for Israel in the wake of the failure of the two wars against Rome (66–70 and 132–135 CE). Their emphasis was on sanctification through order rather than salvation by means of militant human action; hence the challenge to fashion a life-style that could ignore the vicissitudes of history. Yet the memories of history, especially sorrowful ones, do not die easily. By the fourth century, and possibly in reaction to a triumphant Christianity now in charge of the empire, Israel's sages turned back to history in order to learn its lessons for the present. One can decipher the answers in the Talmud of the Land of Israel (Yerushalmi): Israel can never be autonomous; there is only a choice of master – God or the nations. Once this lesson had been learned, the Messiah myth could return, as it does in this great collective work. However, the role of the Messiah is changed in line with the fundamental philosophy developed by the Mishnah earlier – the Messiah is not the agent who will initiate human change, but the sage who will instruct Israel, thus allowing God to achieve God's purpose for Israel, namely sanctification rather than liberation.

These same questions surface again in the writings of the great Jewish philosopher, Maimonides, in the twelfth century. According to Marcel

Poorthuis, a confident belief in the coming of the Messiah was one of his thirteen principles of Jewish faith. Yet Maimonides distanced himself from popular beliefs and expectations. For him the messianic age was a time of freedom for the study of the Torah. When such freedom was achieved the world did not need to be fully Jewish, provided adherents of the other religions (for him Islam and Christianity) converted from idolatry and behaved in a thoroughly moral way. Then all can share in messianic peace in this world. There is a strong political component in Maimonides' expectation of the Messiah, who is thought of as a worldly ruler with real power on behalf of Israel, unlike the apolitical figure of the earlier rabbinic corpus as outlined by Neusner. Yet Maimonides, too, had learned the lessons of history, and he issued strong condemnations of precipitated messianic movements and revolutionary actions, warning against false pretenders.

In sharp contrast with this 'rationalistic' messianism of Maimonides is that espoused by Shabbetai Zevi (1626–1676). The contribution of Marcus van Loopik shows how this was rooted in Jewish mysticism, especially as this had been developed by Yizhaq Luria (1534–1572). Radical transformation of existence and complete rupture with the past was envisaged as part of the messianic age, which was considered not as some distant future event, but as something which could be ushered in now through human action.

The German Reformation provides an interesting illustration of these two tendencies from within the Christian tradition, as Helga Robinson-Hammerstein's learned article demonstrates. On the one hand the doctrine of the two kingdoms allowed Luther to make a sharp distinction between all human efforts in this world which are marked by human sinfulness and the kingdom of God which will be realized at Christ's second coming. The fact that these two can never be merged in Luther's view explains his castigation of the false prophets as he sees them, who attempted to bring about the messianic age through radical action now on the basis of a misguided literalism in their interpretation of the scriptural prophecies. Foremost among these radicals was Thomas Müntzer, whose radical millenarianism was the direct result of his belief in the power of God's word now to transform people's lives. It was this belief that led him increasingly to adopt a revolutionary stance with regard to the social conditions that he encountered on his travels. For him the option of waiting for the Messiah was transformed into a militant call for action based on the apocalyptic understanding of history and fuelled by hopes and dreams still alive in late mediaeval piety.

In the final section some contemporary issues are explored in the light of an ongoing messianic consciousness, even of a secular kind. The editors were forced to choose from many possible topics since the messianic idea has pervaded every aspect of Western thinking in one way or another, even when this is not explicitly recognized. The three topics chosen suggest themselves for rather obvious reasons in the light of the foregoing biblical and historical investigations. A secular reception of belief in the Messiah within Marxism would simply demonstrate how the idea continued to stimulate human imagination in every epoch of Western history; the retrieval of the messianic career of Jesus as this is depicted in the Gospels is at once the stimulus and the contribution of liberation theology, especially in Latin America; the ongoing differences between Jews and Christians already clearly seen in the biblical section continue to be a stumbling block for fruitful dialogue between these two world religions today. All three issues call for urgent discussion and clarification.

For Alistair Kee the question of messianic influences in Marxism should rather be reframed in terms of the challenge that the messianic hopes of that philosophy pose to traditional Western religion which has lost sight of those foundational hopes of its own tradition. The most important premises of Marx's philosophy derive from the Jewish and Christian heritage in which he himself was formed, the author claims. Such basic concepts as freedom, the classless society and the internal moral goal of history have been developed against the background of the biblical doctrine of redemption from injustice and oppression by a subject who transcends all human efforts. Such a Credo or Manifesto is based not on science or fact but on faith, whereby Marx was able to view the events of history in a very different light from what they appeared to be. Thus Marx's messianic faith points to embarrassing gaps in Christian messianic faith.

It is the need for a reawakening of that Christian messianic faith that Jon Sobrino calls to our attention. He contrasts the experiences of the poor of the Third World with those of people living in the First World under the influence of prevailing socio-economic theories of human progress. The poor urgently require the utopian belief in someone whose very existence is caring and who will liberate them from the evils they are experiencing, someone who will inaugurate a reign of justice and peace. Classical Christian thinking about Jesus has divorced his person from the message he has to mediate and led to the postponement to an indefinite future of the kingdom of righteousness that he proclaimed. The delay in the completion of his mission in no way detracts from the definite character of his initial coming. Sobrino calls for a remessianization of Jesus, not in any triumphalistic sense but in order to restore the balance between the mediator and the mediation which has been lost. Only in this way can justice be done to Jesus himself and to the poor who are the first sharers of his destiny and the privileged addressees of his ministry.

Rosemary Radford Ruether's article points to another area where the distortions of Christian messianic claims have had sad consequences, namely relations with Jewish sisters and brothers. She raises the question as to whether it is possible for Christians to proclaim Jesus as the Christ in such a way that they will cease to vilify the Jewish experience of faith and even foster common hopes for a Messiah who will realize God's reign on earth. This can only be achieved when the idea of the Messiah is not separated from God's triumph over all evil in history and with it the retrieval of the Pauline notion of the ingrafting of the church of the Gentiles into Israel, rather than seeing it as the replacement for Israel. In order to begin the process of healing the wounds of Christian anti-Judaism, the old paradigms of replacement/superiority in Christian theological thinking need to be abandoned. The messianic status of Jesus should be seen as contextual and proleptic, in anticipation of the transformation of the world. We Christians share this hope with the Jewish people, even though the name of Jesus has not become for them a paradigmatic expression of its content. Both Jews and Christians are, however, called together to discern the signs of the times in the light of their common appeal to the messianic idea and the shared responsibility to be critical of those movements or events which trade off that hope while at the same time causing oppression and injustice to others.

Seán Freyne

I · Biblical

Did Israel Need the Messiah?

Wim Beuken

The title of this article poses a challenge to an Old Testament scholar. It indicates that its readership will be composed of representatives of other theological disciplines, scholars engaged in the New Testament and the context in which it is set, i.e. the literature of the Second Temple. In these disciplines the terms Messiah and messianism stand for complicated issues, as the following articles in this issue of *Concilium* will indicate. But Old Testament scholars themselves will react in perplexity to the question 'Did Israel need the Messiah?' Their preference is to postpone an answer for the moment and to begin with a description of the term 'anointed', the real meaning of 'Messiah', and a survey of the texts which relate to it. Perhaps to the disappointment of some readers, such a description will show that on this point the language of the Old Testament is very different from that of the New. Gaining insight into the connection between the two Testaments within the one Scripture may very well require considerable effort.

The word 'Messiah' goes back to the Hebrew *mashiach*, 'anointed'. This almost always occurs in the phrase 'YHWH's anointed'. So it is a theological term, one peculiar to Israel, since Israel's oldest neighbours did not know any comparable title. It now belongs in a very specific tradition, that of the election of David and his descendants. We find it predominantly in I and II Samuel and in a number of psalms about the king in Jerusalem. The application of the title to the high priest (Leviticus, and Daniel 9.25f.), the patriarchs (Ps. 105.15) and the Persian king Cyrus (Isa. 45.1) is of marginal significance.

It is assumed that the term 'Yahweh's anointed' is a product of the theological foundation of the Davidic monarchy, as it came into being under Solomon. It is of course based on the tradition of the anointing of David and his descendants king (an anointing which was also projected on to Saul). The nucleus of the accounts of this is older, but there will have been an interaction between them and the term 'YHWH's anointed'. So we may begin with these stories and the way they are reflected in the Psalms (I) in order to trace the meaning of the term (II). After a survey of other Old Testament texts in which the figure of David has assumed such traits that the messianic expectation can be attached to him (III) there finally follows an answer to the question raised in the title (IV). This provides a link with subsequent articles.

I. Anointed king

The stories about the anointing of David, his descendants and his predecessor Saul as king indicate their relative independence of the title 'YHWH's anointed' by the way in which we encounter two sacral juridical models in them. First, it is the elders of the people who carry out the anointing (II Sam. 2.4, 7; 5.2; cf. II Sam. 19.11; I Kings 5.15; II Kings 9.6; 11.12; 23.30), and secondly, the anointing in the name of YHWH is done through the mediation of his prophet or the priest (I Sam. 16.3, 12f.; II Sam. 12.7; cf. I Sam. 9.16; 10.1; 15.1; I Kings 1.34–39, 45). The first conception is that the ruler is set apart from the profane sphere by anointing and put in an unassailable position in order to be a mediator between the people and God, one who guarantees blessing. In the second he embodies God's claim to recognition as Israel's sole ruler and lawgiver. We must take care that modern views do not lead us to see an irreconcilable contradiction between these conceptions of the nature of authority. Rather, both of them were concerned with a unique tension in the Old Testament concept of the king from the house of David and thus 'the anointed'. As a result, on the one hand this concept could be dissociated from the ancient Near Eastern conception of the kingship, which tended towards the identification of the ruler with God, and on the other it could survive the downfall of the state and even of the institution of the monarchy. The king from the house of David was utterly human, subject to God's law and the word of his prophets. At the same time he bore the spirit of YHWH and embodied God's nearness and faithfulness (Deut. 17.14–20; I Sam. 10.6, 9–13; 16.13).

So far, we have left one prophetic story out of account. However, it is the *magna carta* of the theology of kingship in Israel: Nathan's oracle (II Sam. 7.1–17). David's proposal to build a house for YHWH is coupled by God with the promise that he himself will build a house for David, in other words descendants on whom the royal power will rest for ever. In this prophecy it is of great importance that YHWH will punish any injustice on the part of David's descendants, but he will never withdraw his loving kindness (vv. 14f.). In the final sentence of the passage this theology outlines its deepest foundation: 'And your house and your kingdom shall be made sure for ever before me; your throne shall be established for ever' (v. 16). It is important to recognize the prophetic roots of this promise to David. Despite its links in principle to the law of YHWH, the monarchy in Jerusalem was evidently not seen as something which was commensurate with its obedience to the law. At the same time it signified the unshakable faithfulness of YHWH to his people, a faithfulness which was not dependent on their obedience (v. 10). How these two characteristics together made history forms the marvellous guidance of the house of David by YHWH.

Because the prophetic image of the Davidic monarchy is composed of these elements, there is no contradiction in the image of it that we find in the royal psalms (above all Psalms 2; 72; 89, 110). Over the last century a good deal of work has been done to trace the language and the imagery of these texts and the ritual behind them, the so-called royal ideology. It is now clear that Israel began to venerate the relatively new institution of the monarchy with forms of words and rites which abundantly drew on an age-old wealth of material from among neighbouring peoples, above all Egypt. Specialists took some time to assess these borrowings on their own merits. The claims of the monarchy of the world powers Egypt and Assyria were hardly appropriate to the insignificant position of the minor people of Israel. Statements like, 'Ask of me, and I will make the nations your heritage, and the ends of the earth your possession. You shall break them with a rod of iron, and dash them in pieces like a potter's vessel' (Ps. 2.8f.), have been branded a 'political and military day-dream' and the 'flattery of court theologians'. Now we take a different view. The court style of the ancient Near East was a welcome and admirable means of expressing the highest expectations of the prophetic movement about God's faithfulness and his plans for the royal house. As Gerhard von Rad aptly put it, the singers of the royal psalms address the historical monarchy from the perspective of the divine image of it that they had in mind, in other words their prophetic spirit. Therefore they could work in not only the wretched political reality but also the moral fiasco of the house of David. No matter how deep the disappointment over the historical manifestation of this dynasty nor how long it lasted, the promise of YHWH, made through the mouth of the prophet Nathan, gave a guarantee that one day things would change. That did not make the pain of the present any less sharp. One need only read Psalm 89 to see that belief in the promise to David (vv. 19–37 [Hebrew 20–38]), anchored in the order of creation (vv. 1–18 [Hebrew 1–19]), led to doubt about its validity in the present time (vv. 46–51 [Hebrew 47–52]). The psalmist certainly does not himself rediscover his equilibrium within the psalm. But the fact that the confession and the lament stand side by side is enough indication of the tension in the theology of the anointed.

The conclusion to be drawn from all this is that even before the exile, the Davidic tradition developed into, and indeed really from the beginning functioned as, a paradigm for the expectation that YHWH would eventually realize fully the salvation that he had promised through an offspring from this house. Of course people can argue endlessly over the question whether this expectation was originally eschatological. The answer depends on how one defines eschatological. If one wants to include in the definition the element of an end to historical time, then the Old Testament expectation of the anointed was not eschatological. But if one gives full weight to the element of the complete and irrevocable realization of the promise, then the expectation of the true son of David is one of the spiritual forces which bear witness to the Name down to the period of the Second Temple and from then on down to our own time.

II. 'YHWH's anointed'

Now that we have surveyed to some extent the historical background to the theme of 'David and his descendants' and its literary expression, the time has come to take stock of the concept of 'YHWH's anointed', of course within its Old Testament contours.

First of all, it is striking that this title encompasses the books of I and II Samuel. When Hannah sets her son Samuel apart for the service of YHWH, she ends her song of thanksgiving to God for having delivered her from barrenness with the words: 'YHWH will judge the ends of the earth; he will give strength to his king, and exalt the power of his anointed' (I Sam. 2.10). The phrase 'his king/his anointed' is, of course, an anachronism, for Samuel is the very person who will institute the monarchy in Israel. However, as a redactional programme for I and II Samuel this announcement is very skilful. These books are about the establishment of the monarchy in Israel by YHWH, about Saul's failure (I Samuel) and David's success (II Samuel). Moreover, 'the last words of David' are also announced as 'the oracle of David . . . the anointed of the God of Jacob' (II Sam. 23.1). This was the focus of Samuel's prophetic activity: the foundation of a kingship which was not just like 'that among all the nations' (I Sam. 8.5) but a kingship which could take the word of YHWH explicitly as the criterion for a 'just ruler over men, ruling in the fear of God' (II Sam. 23.3). So David's last confession amounts to an indication by the redactor that Hannah's prophetic words to this king are going to be fulfilled. It emerges that, in the kingdom that he has been able to found, God judges the earth by giving strength to his anointed. According to the song of thanksgiving which precedes the last words of David, this kingdom is also the proof of God's faithfulness towards his anointed (II Sam. 22.51). In this sense Hannah's words comprise a programme for what Israel continues to expect down the centuries from the house of David.

If we investigate further the significance of the title 'YHWH's anointed' in I–II Samuel, it emerges that in the majority of passages David is referring to himself, not to establish his own prerogatives but the inviolability of Saul and his life (I Sam. 24.7, 11; 26.9, 11, 16, 23) and to punish any infringement (II Sam. 1.14, 16). We may see this, too, as an anachronism. The narrator puts the title in David's mouth long before the royal theology from the time of Solomon was to create it. His intention was probably to depict David's historical rival as his predecessor, willed by God but rejected. There is no better picture of the unassailable position enjoyed by the son of David, installed with divine authority, than the demonstration that the ancestor of this family had respected his opponent, even when the strategic situation gave him the opportunity of doing away with him and his comrade-in-arms Abishai gave him the justification: 'Today God has delivered your enemy into your hand' (I Sam. 26.8).

The other passages in I–II Samuel in which the title 'YHWH's anointed' occurs are sparse, but they fill in some details. In the first place, the anointed is God's own choice, and here the decisive element is not found in human norms of appearance and form but in the reaction of the heart. That becomes evident when the sons of Jesse are presented to Samuel. Even Samuel is mistaken in his expectation of God's choice (I Sam. 16.6), which is David, the youngest, who is not there (vv. 11–12). Secondly, Samuel himself indicates where the real task of the anointed lies by calling Saul as well as YHWH to be witness to his upright life as he bids farewell to the people of Israel (I Sam. 12.3, 5). Here he indicates what must be a fundamental trait of the character of the anointed, of course in contrast to the actual conduct of the house of David. Instead of protecting justice within Israel, the kings have often brought shame on themselves by enriching themselves at the cost of their subjects. The most telling contrast

to I Samuel 12, where Saul bears witness to Samuel's impeccable life
(v. 3: 'Whose ox have I taken? . . . Whom have I defrauded? Whom have I
oppressed?'), is the story of how King Ahab illegally appropriated
Naboth's vineyard and his wife contrived false witness against Naboth
(I Kings 21). Finally, one might refer to II Sam. 19.22, where David sets
mercy above law in the case of the man who has cursed one who is
YHWH's anointed.

Thus the books of I and II Samuel paint a picture of the anointed with
firm lines. His choice is God's own decision, which people must honour by
never laying hands on him, in other words by allowing YHWH to have
complete control over him. He guarantees law and justice in Israel, but lets
mercy prevail when his own interest is involved. We can now understand
how the house of David could survive its own fall at the destruction of
Jerusalem only under this cipher of the ideal descendant, and embody the
coming of God's kingdom even after the exile.

It is significant that the title 'YHWH's anointed' in I and II Samuel has
no role at all in I and II Kings. What does this silence tell us? It fits
admirably with the fact that these books of the Bible in particular bring out
the religious and moral failings of the house of David.

The book of Psalms, and above all the royal psalms, add other features to
the picture of 'YHWH's anointed'. More than in I and II Samuel, here he
emerges as the defender of his people against foreign rulers. In this
function he enjoys the support of YHWH (Ps. 18.51; 20.7; cf. Hab. 3.13)
and becomes the legal basis for redemption (Ps. 84.10; 132.10, 17) and
mediator of salvation (Ps. 28.8). His bond with God amounts to the
uniqueness of a personal covenant (Ps. 89.3, 28, 35 [Hebrew 4, 29, 36]; cf.
II Sam. 23.5). At the same time YHWH's anointed accentuates the aporia
of the downfall of the monarchy, for when God's wrath indeed comes upon
Israel, the conclusion must be that YHWH has turned even against his
anointed (Lam. 4.20). Psalm 89 is illuminating here. The lament contains
the lofty saying: 'But now you have cast off and rejected, you are full of
wrath against your anointed. You have renounced the covenant with your
servant; you have defiled his crown in the dust' (vv. 38ff. [Hebrew 39ff.]).
Then comes the question about God's faithfulness: 'Lord, where is your
steadfast love of old, which by your faithfulness you did swear to David?'
(v. 49 [Hebrew v. 50]). Only at the end of the psalm does the king, the
anointed, himself speak: 'Remember, Lord, how your servant is scorned,
how I bear in my bosom the insults of the peoples, with which your
enemies taunt, YHWH, with which they mock the footsteps of your
anointed' (vv. 50f. [Hebrew vv. 51f.]). There is no space in this article to

analyse the subtle terminology of this last verse, but here it emerges clearly that at a time of great need the anointed stands among his oppressed people, and implies that the shame also affects YHWH because YHWH involves himself (cf. the explicit statement in Ps. 2.2: 'The rulers rise up against YHWH and his anointed'). Here he is mediator from the people to God, on the basis of the interest that he shares with God.

So the royal psalms provide a not unimportant supplement to the picture of the anointed in I–II Samuel. He holds YHWH and his people together when the people complain about YHWH. Therefore the conflagration will finally result not only in salvation for Israel but also in recognition of the king on Zion, whom YHWH has made his son (Ps. 2.6–7).

III. The interpretation of David and his house after the exile

The texts that we have discussed so far form a history of the interpretation of the historical fact of David and the tradition about him. Alongside this, within the Old Testament itself another form of interpretation came into being, the interpretation of these texts about David himself. We must also pay attention to these. This spiritual movement, which is very closely connected with the experience of the exile, forms the last stage on our way to the messianism which lies beyond the horizon of the Old Testament.

It is particularly instructive to see how the Chronicler (I Chron. 17.1–15) shifts the meaning of Nathan's oracle (II Sam. 7.17). Central to the first text is the promise that YHWH will build a house, i.e. a dynasty, for David. For the Chronicler, that is already in the past (vv. 7–10 must be translated as a retrospect). His interest lies in the house that David's son will build for YHWH (v. 12). In this framework the eternal duration of the house of David also takes on another perspective. Whereas in the first text the narrator tries to fit the moral failings of the house of David into this absolute guarantee (II Sam. 7.14–16), the Chronicler is silent about it. Moreover, he transforms the eternal rule of the house of David into a permanent function in the house and kingdom of YHWH himself: 'I will confirm him in my house and in my kingdom for ever and his throne shall be established for ever' (I Chron. 7.14). On the one hand the kingdom of David's house is here reduced to a theocratic task, and on the other the son of David in this view is indissolubly bound up with the kingdom of YHWH himself.

It is not certain that here the Chronicler has opened up the way to a messianic interpretation of the promise to David. The question is how much room there is in his view of the post-exilic temple community for an eschatological future. That question goes beyond the bounds of this article. The Chronicler's reinterpretation simply shows that the tradition about David and his house was very much on the move at the end of the Old Testament period, and moreover that this cipher was slowly incorporated into the theologoumenon of the kingdom of God.

At the same time we must note that this reinterpretation of the son of David does not take up the title 'YHWH's anointed'. This striking omission also emerges in other texts which are regarded as later interpretations of earlier texts about the expected shoot from the house of David. Here we come up against one of the anomalies about the connection between the Old Testament and the later messianic expectation. This discrepancy is all the more striking because one cannot identify any cause or reason for it. It is impossible to discuss these texts further within the compass of this article. I simply add a list: Isa. 9.1–6 on the child from the house of David with the exalted names who will bring peace and justice; Isa. 11.1–10 on the shoot from the stem of Jesse who will be the bearer of God's spirit *par excellence*; Amos 9.11–15 on the restoration of the fallen hut of David; Micah 5.1–3 on the ruler who will arise from Bethlehem; Zech. 6.12 on the Branch who will rebuild the temple of YHWH (cf. Jer. 23.5–8). Each of these texts needs thorough investigation if we are to establish in a responsible way whether and to what degree the abiding role of the house of David has eschatological dimensions in the mediation of salvation and consequently the passage can be called messianic. But it is in any case the fact that the concept of 'YHWH's anointed' is missing, along with all that this presupposes.

IV. Messianic without Messiah?

We have surveyed as far as possible within the space available Old Testament texts which may have some messianic connotations. We covered not only the texts which speak explicitly about the anointing of the king and 'YHWH's anointed' but also texts which in one way or another assign a role to the house of David in the coming of salvation. That makes all the more pressing the question why we leave out of account texts which are interpreted as messianic in the New Testament and the intertestamental literature. This is a great and important arsenal. It is useful to give some indication of it:

– The enmity between the woman and the serpent and between their seed in Gen. 3.15 is the basis for the enmity between the woman who has given birth to a male child and the dragon in Revelation 12.

– In the Targum Onkelos the difficult words in the blessing of Judah, 'until Shiloh comes and the people are obedient to him' (Gen. 49.10), are translated: 'until the Messiah comes, to whom the kingdom belongs'. Similarly, in the same Targum Balaam's remark, 'A star arises from David, a sceptre rises upon Israel' (Num. 24.17), is translated: 'When a king from Jacob shall arise and the anointed of Israel shall be exalted'.

– The prophecy of Immanuel (Isa. 7.14), which in its own context refers either to the son of King Ahaz or to the son of Isaiah (there is no consensus over this), is applied by Matthew (1.23) to Jesus in a messianic perspective.

– When Jesus settles in Capernaum, the same evangelist (4.13–16) sees this as the fulfilment of the prophecy of Isa. 8.23–9.1: 'The land of Zebulun and the land of Napthali, towards the sea, across the Jordan, Galilee of the Gentiles – the people who sat in darkness have seen a great light.'

When Paul defends himself by saying that he did not begin to proclaim 'the name of Christ (anointed!)' where that had already happened, he refers to the prophecy of the suffering servant: 'They shall see who have never been told of him, and they shall understand who have never heard of him' (Rom. 15.21; cf. Isa. 52.15).

This arbitrary selection could be supplemented by many other references. (I have not once mentioned texts from the literature of the Second Temple period and the discoveries from the Dead Sea.) It emerges from all this material that around the beginning of our era a paradigm had developed in which on the one hand the coming salvation of God was interpreted eschatologically, and on the other it was bound up with the mediation of a figure who in principle comes from the house of David, but sometimes has also integrated features of other typical bringers of salvation, like Moses, the servant of YHWH from Isaiah and the Son of Man from Daniel. It is this eschatological figure who is subsequently called 'the Messiah'.

We do not find this notion in the Old Testament. The fullness of salvation here is not necessarily eschatological, i.e. it does not necessarily put an end to history. It does not necessarily come through the mediation of a suffering figure, and even where such a figure *is* part of the eschatological scheme, it is not necessarily someone from the house of David, an 'anointed'. The inauguration of God's rule, for example, is not bound up with a human figure (Psalms 47; 93; 95–9). Moreover, the servant of YHWH in Deutero-Isaiah and the Son of Man in Daniel 7 are not presented as shoots from the house of David. In short, the integration

of different saviour figures in one Messiah and the far-reaching sys-
tematization of expectations of salvation in Messianism fall outside the
limits of the Old Testament.

Against the background of these findings I shall now try to give an
answer to the question which forms the title of this article: 'Did Israel need
the Messiah?' That is not an easy task. First we have to make it clear what
'Israel' means here. If one means by it the community of faith of the
Second Temple, 'the Messiah' embodies its need for redemption. At least
this Israel thought that it needed the Messiah. Whether Jesus endorsed this
conception is another question.

We can also see 'Israel' as the community of faith which speaks in the Old
Testament seen as normative scripture. This manifestation of Israel is of
course difficult to distinguish from the one that I have just mentioned, and
knew the same need for redemption. This Israel expressed its expectation
in a variety of ciphers: the new exodus, the true Son of David, the covenant
written in the heart, the light from Zion. These are not integrated into o ne
system, into a metaphorical construction or a doctrine of the coming and
the nature of definitive salvation. The writing prophets each use only a
particular selection of these great themes in their preaching. In principle
one can be missing, even that of the son of David, although this theme was
very widespread, albeit without the specific term 'the anointed'.

The question now gradually becomes: did Old Testament Israel need its
son of David – let us call him 'the anointed'? It remains a strange but useful
question. This community urgently needed redemption, so much so that
the question of mediation cannot be raised apart from it. The pledge of this
redemption, the saving facts which brought it about, were as necessary as
the redemption itself. When the sea threatens to break in, all emergency
measures are needed. The ciphers shared in the absolute value of what they
signified. Together they embodied the seriousness of both the experience
of need and the promise of redemption.

After this necessarily qualified answer to the question which forms the
title of this article, the following prayer therefore has ultimate validity: 'O
Lord God, do not turn away the face of your anointed one! Remember
your steadfast love for David your servant!' (II Chron. 6.42).

Translated by John Bowden

Select bibliography

Books
S. Mowinckel, *He That Cometh*, Oxford 1956
T. N. D. Mettinger, *King and Messiah*, Coniectanea Biblica, Old Testament 8, Lund 1976
J. Becker, *Messiaserwartung im Alten Testament*, Stuttgarter Bibelstudien 83, Stuttgart 1977
H. Cazelles, *Le Messie de la Bible. Christologie de l'Ancien Testament*, Tournai and Paris 1978
U. Struppe (ed.), *Studien zum Messiasbild im Alten Testament*, Stuttgarter Biblische Aufsatzbände 6, Stuttgart 1989

Articles
Gerhard von Rad, 'Erwägungen zu den Königspsalmen', *Zeitschrift für die alttestamentliche Wissenschaft* 58, 1940–41, 216–22
A. S. van der Woude, 'De oorsprong van Israëls Messiaanse Verwachtingen', *Kerk en Theologie* 24, 1973, 1–11
Ernst-Joachim Waschke, 'Die Frage nach dem Messias im Alten Testament als Problem alttestamentlicher Theologie und biblischer Hermeneutik', *Theologische Literaturzeitung* 113, 1988, 321–32
R. E. Clements, 'The Messianic Hope in the Old Testament', *Journal for the Study of the Old Testament* 43, 1989, 3–19

Palestinian Jewish Groups and Their Messiahs in Late Second Temple Times

Richard Horsley

Contrary to traditional Christian claims, most Jews at the time of Jesus were clearly not waiting for the arrival of the Messiah. The very concept of 'the Messiah' is a product of Christian theological reflection. Early Christians drew on several different traditions, some of them from the Hebrew Bible and/or the Septuagint, of historical or anticipated future agents of deliverance in their attempts to express the significance of Jesus. Gradually the many different images and traditions were con-fused into a highly synthetic and dominating concept of 'Christ'. That concept, in turn, had a decisive and formative effect on both the modern popular and scholarly construction of the Jewish expectation of 'the Messiah'. What Christians claim to have 'found' in Jesus determined what Christians claimed had been prophesied by Israelite prophets and/or expected by the Jews.

As a topic of discussion in modern theology, in fact, 'the Messiah' is also part of a larger conceptual apparatus of Christian origins that has little to do with the lives of the people of ancient Palestine. We continue to write and talk about 'early Christianity' as a 'religious' community that started as a 'reform movement' within 'Judaism', thought of as a 'religion' or a larger 'religious' community. It is becoming increasingly clear, however, that it is difficult to locate and identify historical realities to which these concepts might refer. As we discern the dramatic differences between the different writings in the New Testament, we are realizing that several different communities of Jesus-followers sprang up within a few decades both in

Palestine and in the larger Hellenistic-Roman world, none of which defined themselves over-against 'the Jews' or 'Israel'.

The standard old scholarly concept of 'Judaism' was based largely on evidence from rabbinic literature that originated from two to five centuries after Jesus and the destruction of the temple in Jerusalem. But to speak of 'Judaism' or 'Jewish sects' in order to recognize the diversity in first-century Jewish Palestine is equally unsatisfactory. Identifiable groups in Palestine, such as Pharisees and Sadducees, were not merely religious communities analogous to modern 'sects' such as Baptists or Mennonites over against the 'established religion.' What modern Westerners call 'religion' is embedded with other dimensions of life, such as the political and economic and even kinship in virtually any traditional society, including ancient Palestine. Identifiable groups in ancient Jewish Palestine each had a particular social location and political-economic interest and role which were inseparable from its religious ideals and practices.

Structural social conflict and alternative cultural traditions

The social structure of ancient Judaea, like that of other ancient Near Eastern societies, involved a fundamental division between rulers and ruled.[1] The vast majority of the latter were marginal peasants living in semi-autonomous village and town communities. The rulers, supported by tithes, taxes, and/or rents taken from the peasant producers, formed culturally as well as politically dominant urban communities with their 'retainers' who helped them govern and artisans and others who served their interests. The situation of ancient Jewish Palestine was somewhat similar to that of a 'Third World' people in the modern world subject to an imperial power, in which the dominant families are themselves clients of imperial rulers.[2] Since the sixth century BCE the ancient Judaean people had been ruled by a temple-state sponsored originally by the Persian imperial regime. The temple and its high priesthood continued as the dominant political-economic-religious institution under the successive Hellenistic and Roman empires. Persian imperial policy also favoured the revival and consolidation of subject peoples' legal and cultural traditions. Thus the heads of the Judaean temple-state and their scribal retainers produced the Torah as the 'constitution' and 'laws' of the temple-state and continued the development of the psalms, etc. as key components of the 'liturgy' of the temple.

In order to understand the emergence of longings for liberation, including hopes for a 'messiah' or other agent of deliverance in late second-temple times, we must grasp both the potential social structural conflicts inherent in the ancient imperial situation, particularly the mediating role of scribes and other retainers, and their special attachment to the cultural traditions of Judaea. That is, like the rulers of other traditional ancient Near Eastern societies, the Judaean high priests governed their subjects with the assistance of scribal retainers. These scribal officials, familiar to us in late second-temple times as 'scribes' and Pharisees, were responsible for cultivating, interpreting and applying the Torah and/or other legal and cultural traditions. So long as the high-priestly rulers remained reasonably comfortable in the traditional culture and laws, inherent structural tensions were manageable through the mediation of the scribal retainers (see, e.g., Sirach 38.24–39.5). But when the high-priestly rulers departed from the traditional ways – and, in the Hellenizing reform of 175 BCE and after, even programmatically assimilated to the dominant imperial culture – then the scribes were placed in an acute conflict of loyalties between the traditions they were responsible for cultivating and interpreting and the rulers for whom they worked and on whom they were politically-economically dependent.[3]

In order to understand why certain Judaean groups might utilize an image of a *messiah* in their hopes, it is also important to recognize that the cultural heritage of the temple-state contained traditions that challenged the power and privilege of the rulers as well as traditions that legitimated their dominant position, and that symbolism of 'anointed' was involved in both cases.

Once the Davidic monarchy had established itself in the orginally non-Israelite city of Jerusalem, it had legitimated itself with an ideology of divinely ordained kingship borrowed from ancient Near Eastern mythology of imperial monarchy.[4] This exalted royal ideology is articulated in several 'royal psalms' such as Psalms 2, 89, 110, as well as in God's 'covenant' with David, in II Samuel 7. It includes such elements as the divine 'only-begotten' sonship ('You are my son; today I have begotten you', Ps. 2.7), the promise of perpetual or eternal continuation of the Davidic dynasty ('I will establish the throne of his kingdom forever', II Sam 7.13; cf. Ps. 132.11–12), and the sacral dimension of the kingship ('You are a priest for ever according to the order of Melchizedek', Ps. 110.4). This ideology of imperial monarchy continued in official prophetic oracles delivered on the occasion of the birth of royal sons, such as that in Isa. 9.2–7.

David himself, however, had originally been a popular king, not an oriental monarch. Having made his start as a prominent warrior under another popular king, Saul, and then as a bandit-chief served the enemy Philistines, David was popularly acclaimed or 'anointed' as king first by his own tribe of Judahites and then by the elders of all Israel (II Sam. 2.4; 5.1–3). Once he transformed his kingship into an established monarchy in the Jebusite city of Jerusalem, of course, he had to conquer the rebellious Israelites with his own non-Israelite mercenary troops (II Sam. 15–20). But the tradition remained that David had had his start as a king who had been 'anointed' by the people themselves as their leader against foreign domination by the Philistines. That tradition of popularly anointed kingship continued among the northern tribes who broke away from the Davidic monarchy at the death of Solomon, with successive popular insurrections led by figures such as Jeroboam and Jehu. It appears that the tradition of popular kingship functioned as a counter to the mythologized ideology of imperial kingship.

Parallel to and supportive of the tradition of popular kingship, in its opposition to imperial monarchy and its mythic legitimation, were other Israelite traditions, particularly those of the exodus and the Mosaic covenant. In its very origins the people of Israel was a people who had escaped from alien domination in Egypt. And the Mosaic covenant and its attendant mechanisms of sabbatical release of debts and slaves articulated egalitarian political-economic principles as the will of the God who had originally liberated the Israelites from foreign rule. Both oracular prophets such as Amos and Jeremiah and prophets who led resistance movements among the people, such as Elijah and Elisha, reasserted the Mosaic covenantal principles against the systematic exploitation by the established monarchy and its officials.

In the establishment of the temple-state in the sixth and fifth centuries BCE, however, the ideology of anointed kingship was first relativized and then, in effect, abandoned. The founding ideal articulated by the prophet Zechariah and others was a diarchy or 'double rule' of an anointed priest and an anointed Davidic prince (Zerubbabel). But gradually the high priesthood simply displaced the remnants of the monarchy. The high priesthood had become so thoroughly and exclusively entrenched as the model of societal leadership by the early second century BCE[5] that the first several generations of rebellion against the incumbents could think only in terms of another high priesthood (Hasmonaeans) or of direct action by God himself (early Enoch literature; Daniel) or some combination of the two (most of the Dead Sea Scrolls). Only gradually did dissident groups reach for alternative images of leadership, such as a Davidic messiah (Psalms of Solomon). Most of our evidence, of course, in so far as we are dependent on literature, comes from 'intellectual' strata, i.e., groups of dissident scribal retainers. Through the Jewish historian Josephus, however, we also have windows on to a few popular movements which did not simply imagine an alternative state of affairs but took concrete action.

Ideologies of the intellectuals

In the early second century BCE, a powerful circle among the ruling priesthood and their wealthy non-priestly allies gained the imperial favour of the Seleucid regime and engineered a transformation of the society into Hellenistic forms, culturally as well as politically. In so far as the traditional Torah and/or Mosaic covenantal institutions were replaced by Hellenistic political-religious forms, the scribal retainers were left without a social-political role and economic support. Eventually the scribes/sages led and/or joined a popular revolt against the Hellenizing Reform carried out by their (former) priestly patrons. But prior to the outright persecution of the faithful *maskilim* (Daniel 11.33), groups of scribes began articulating their disillusionment with the high priesthood as well as their opposition to their rulers and their imperial allies. The early texts, Daniel and the early Enoch literature, contain no motif whatever of a *messiah*. The only alternative to high-priestly leadership was action by God himself or by some combination of God, angelic beings, and/or the righteous themselves. As the Hasmonaean family consolidated its power on the strength of Judas the Maccabee's and his brothers' leadership of the 'Maccabean' revolt, they set themselves up as a restored high priesthood. There is virtually no indication in the extant texts of any interest in a *messiah* until well after the disillusionment with that restoration, in the texts found at Qumran.

I Enoch[6]

The early 'Enoch literature' appears to have been produced by a circle of scribes/sages during the first several decades of the second century BCE. Four of the five major sections of the book of I Enoch were found among the Dead Sea Scrolls, although there is no reason to believe that they were written by the community at Qumran. The authors are likely to have been (former) scribal retainers of the temple government in Jerusalem alienated by the Hellenizing 'reform' and wealthy and powerful ruling circles which they viewed as 'selling out' to Western culture and political forms. Most of this literature is revelation of wisdom that helps the puzzled and suffering righteous ones understand what is happening in the world, and reassuring them that God is ultimately in control. Angels, along with 'Enoch', play the key – one might even say salvific – revelatory roles. Not every section of the book of I Enoch portrays a scene of deliverance. In fact, the principal climax or solution to the distress experienced by the authors appears to be the divine judgment, in which the righteous are vindicated and the oppressive rulers and sinners are condemned. In the first major section, chs. 1–36, God himself is the primary agent of judgment; in The Epistle of Enoch, chs. 92–105, and in the Apocalypse of Weeks, chs. 93.1–10 + 91.12–19, the righteous themselves join in punishment of the sinners/ rulers (95.3; 96.1; 98.12; 93.10; 91.12). Back in the synthetic heyday of identifying every conceivable symbol of redemption as 'messianic', the great white bull of final time of 'heaven on earth' at the end of the Animal Apocalypse (chs. 85–90) was viewed as the Davidic Messiah (Charles, *Enoch*, 215–16). But the white bull, like all the other white bulls, is a symbol of the restoration of the vitality and purity of primordial humanity. Scholarly consensus identifies the 'great horn on one of the sheep' in I Enoch 90.9 as Judas the Maccabee, leader of the revolt against Hellenistic imperial domination. But here as elsewhere in these four sections of I Enoch found at Qumran, there is no mention of any identifiable messianic figure or motif.

Daniel[7]

Those who produced the book of Daniel apparently left their signature in 11.33–35: they were 'the wise among the people', the *maskilim*, who were being martyred for their faithful adherence to the traditional Judaean way of life in the face of imperial military enforcement of the Hellenizing reform. Faced with the 'double-bind' situation either of being killed by the imperial troops if they persisted in their faith or of being abandoned by God if they acquiesced in the reform, and thus desperate for some assurance that God was still in control of history, these *maskilim* sought revelation in dreams and visions. The result was the series of visions in Daniel 7–12, revelations which introduced two symbols which became highly influential among subsequent generations of Jews and then Christians who faced similarly oppressive circumstances. These apocalyptic visions, like most subsequent ones, carry a fundamental three-fold message: God, being indeed ultimately in control of historical events, will (*a*) judge the oppressive imperial and/or domestic rulers; (*b*) restore or renew the people now undergoing persecution or other forms of oppression to a free life under their own and God's sovereignty ('kingdom of God'); and (*c*) vindicate those who are martyred for the faith prior to the judgment of the oppressors and liberation of the people. The newly articulated symbol for the vindication of the martyrs, the *resurrection* (in Dan. 12.2–3), became a central article of faith for Palestinian Jews, particularly the Pharisees, and then, through some key groups of Jesus' followers, for what became orthodox Christianity. The most famous and influential symbol for the restoration of the people to (God's and/or their own) sovereignty, as it emerges in the dream imagery of Daniel 7.1–14, was 'one like a son of man' or 'the humanlike one', given sovereignty at the divine judgment, in counterpoise to the ferocious beasts. Although some 'Christian' groups, such as those addressed in the Gospel of Matthew, understood 'the Son of Man' as a title of a redemptive agent, the dream image in Daniel 7.13–14 is clearly and explicitly interpreted as 'the people of the holy ones of the Most High' in 7.18, 27. Thus the image of 'the one like a human, coming with the clouds . . . and given dominion and kingship' was not originally a title of a redemptive figure at all, but a dream image or symbol for the restoration of the whole people to independent life under their divine king. God himself was the agent of judgment and deliverance and vindication (with apparent help from 'the great [angelic] prince, Michael', in 12.1).

The Dead Sea Scrolls

Since there is such a paucity of references to any 'messiah' in Jewish literature around the time of Jesus, a great deal of excitement greeted the appearance of several references to 'the messiah(s) of Aaron and Israel' in two of the scrolls found at Qumran near the Dead Sea in 1947. The scrolls appear to have been left there by a community consisting largely of priests and scribes. The community was formed apparently in reaction against the 'deal' made by the Hasmonaean leaders of the 'Maccabean' revolt with the imperial regime to have themselves recognized as the new high priestly rulers of Judaea – hence the harangues against 'the wicked priests'. The community lasted well into Roman times, however, and fantasized a final cosmic battle of God and the heavenly armies against 'the Kittim', i.e., the Romans who had taken over rule of Palestine. In the Damascus Document, one of the scrolls for community instruction, a stereotyped phrase 'until the coming of/until there shall arise the messiah of Aaron and Israel' occurs several times (CD 12.23; 14.19; 19.9–11; 20.1) in reference to a future point of time until which the community will observe the ordinances given. The one reference in the Community Rule (1QS 9.10–11) is similar but adds a prophetic figure: 'they shall be governed by the original ordinances in which the men of the community were first instructed until the coming of a prophet and the messiahs of Aaron and Israel'. Again in the famous 'messianic banquet' text (1QSa 2), where the term is explicitly only 'the messiah of Israel' but the context again has the Aaronic leader as well, the reference is to the time of fulfilment, the beginning of the new age. No functions, certainly no redemptive or liberative functions, are attributed to 'the messiah(s) of Aaron and Israel'. Their coming or presence simply marks the final arrival of the new age. And the community apparently patterned the duality of their representation as heads of the eschatological people on the ideal of the original founding of the second temple community, which had two 'olive trees', two anointed ones, a priest as well as a prince (Joshua and Zerubbabel; see esp. Zech 4.1–14).

None of the other major scrolls found at Qumran, such as the Hymns and the Temple Scroll (and very few the lesser documents), even contain the term *messiah*. As a community already living in a state of anticipatory fulfilment of history, the Qumran community looked back on leadership of the Righteous Teacher as having major significance. He was the one who, inspired by God, had inaugurated the decisive 'exodus' into the wilderness and the founding of the new 'covenant' community there which was 'preparing the way of the Lord' through study and practice of the Torah. For the completion of the time of fulfilment, for the decisive final battle against the forces of evil, the community looked for leadership to God himself (see esp. the War Scroll, 1QM), just as had both the *maskilim* behind the book of Daniel and the scribes who produced the early Enoch literature. It is safe to say that the Qumranites did not look to their messiahs as agents of deliverance.

On the other hand, the scribal-priestly community spent a good deal of energy studying the scriptures for references to their own time of crisis and fulfilment. Among the texts found are some which, while not necessarily using the explicit term *messiah*, do pick up biblical references to a future king, who stands alongside a future priest and a future prophet. In the interpretation of the Jacob's Blessing of Judah (4Qpatr) from Gen. 49.10, the 'rule' of the whole people Israel has priority, but within that rule of Israel would be present 'the ruler's sceptre, who would be "the messiah of righteousness, the branch of David"'. In a collection of biblical texts understood apparently as prophecies (4Qtest), Deut. 18.18–19, Num. 24.15–17 and Deut. 33.8–11 are understood respectively with reference to a prophet like Moses, the future star/sceptre of Israel, and the future high priest (Levi, teacher of the Torah). The future triumvirate here parallels the reference in 1QS 9.11. Finally, the anthology of biblical texts with commentary (4Qflor) gathers a number of texts often labelled as 'messianic', such as II Sam. 7.10–14, Amos 9.11, and Ps. 2.1. And the Davidic king is indeed present in the interpretation. But interestingly enough the application features (the remnant of) Israel as a whole in the most prominent position, as the 'house' to be established, the 'you' (originally David) to be given rest from oppressive enemies, and even as 'the Lord's anointed' against which the kings of the nations rage. The only reference that has a redemptive role for the Davidic king interprets the 'tent of David' of Amos 9.11 as 'he who is to save Israel'. What these texts appear to indicate is scribal memories of certain biblical texts as referring to a future Davidic king. But the scribes at Qumran, at least, not only attributed little or no significant redemptive role to a Davidic messiah, but took some of those key biblical 'messianic' prophecies as referring instead to the community of Israel as a whole.

Psalms of Solomon

Psalm of Solomon 17 was the source of the classical 'proof-text' for the standard Christian claim that 'the Jews' expected a 'political messiah'. As we shall see, that claim involved a serious misreading of its only possible piece of textual evidence.

The Psalms of Solomon appear to have been produced by a group of scribes/sages sometime after the mid-first century BCE. These psalms have previously been thought of as Pharisaic. But there were non-Pharisee scribal retainers as well, and nothing indicates that Pharisees in particular might have written them. The writers react sharply against both the Hasmonaean high-priestly rulers and the Roman conquest of Jerusalem in 63 BCE. They had apparently been 'driven out' by the last Hasmonaean rulers, whose dynasty in their mind was illegitimate, hence divinely punished by Pompey's invasion (PsSol 2; 17.1–18). They characterize themselves as 'the assemblies of the pious' (17.16), although they are concerned more broadly for 'the assemblies of Israel' as a whole (10.6–7). One has the impression from reading the entire Psalm 17 that these 'pious ones' were harking back to Davidic monarchy as *the* divinely designated rule of Israel (with specific allusion to God's promise to David in II Samuel 7) and totally rejecting the second temple high priesthood as utterly illegitimate because it had 'despoiled the throne of David' (17.4, 6). Thus the solution to the devastation of the land and the malaise of the people under alien Roman rule is for God to raise up a king who is explicitly 'the son of David' and 'messiah'. The anointed Davidic king's role is two-fold: to drive out both destructive foreign and unrighteous domestic rulers, and to restore the people in their land with just political-economic relations (see esp. 17.22–23, 26–28, 36, 41). This anointed Davidic king, however, is conceived in the image of his scribal creators. He is pointedly not an imperial monarch, pointedly neither a military leader nor a ruler exploitative of his subjects (esp. 17.33, 41). His *modus operandi* is to be 'sapiential'. He is to convict, expose, and drive out the arrogant, unrighteous, and oppressive rulers 'by the power *of his word*' (esp. 17.24–25, 35–36). And within Israel he does not reign from a luxurious palace but teaches the people 'in the assemblies' (17.48). Not by the 'sword' but by the 'word'. The messiah of the Psalms of Solomon is, like his creators, clearly not the imperial ruler of the Davidic dynasty originally legitimated in II Samuel 7, but a teacher of Torah.

Similitudes of Enoch

While not found among the Dead Sea Scrolls, the second section of I Enoch, the Similitudes, chs. 37–72, does appear to belong to Jewish apocalyptic literature, dating probably from early- or mid-first century CE. Among the sections of I Enoch, only the 'Similitudes' focus on a transcendent agent besides God as executing judgment. This figure, called interchangeably 'the Elect/Chosen One' and 'that Human(like) One', appears to be the highest-ranking angelic being in the divine court. At one point (46.1), the Elect One is introduced in a vision that closely resembles the vision of 'The Ancient of Days' and 'One like a son of man' in Daniel 7.9–13. At another point (I Enoch 62–63), 'The Chosen One' is represented in terms reminiscent of the last Servant Song of Second Isaiah (Isa. 53), at yet another (49.2) he is portrayed as having the same 'spirit of wisdom and spirit of insight' as the righteous Davidic king prophesied in Isa. 11.2, and the same figure is referred to twice as 'the Righteous One' (38.2; 53.6) and twice as 'the Anointed One' (48.10; 52.4). Clearly the visionaries behind the Similitudes of Enoch have drawn upon previous tradition of speculation about agents of deliverance. It would be wrong to say that the author here depicts 'the Messiah' . . . 'as a transcendent figure'. The term 'anointed one' is a relatively insignificant reference used in passing only twice in reference to a transcendent figure called 'The Chosen One' and 'The Human One' who is to exercise judgment of the kings and mighty ones from their thrones. Far more important for comparison with 'Christian' speculation about the significance of Jesus, the Similitudes of Enoch provide an example of a roughly contemporary Jewish community engaged in speculation about a transcendent judgment figure referred to as 'that Human(like) One', among a series of fluid 'titles'.

As we know from Gospel texts such as Matthew 25, some Christian groups identified such an angelic judgment figure (the Son of Man) with Jesus (Christ).

IV Ezra and II Baruch[8]

The apocalypse of IV Ezra, shaped into a dialogue through a series of seven visions, was written, around 100 CE, in response to the Roman destruction of the temple and Jerusalem. No reference is made to a messiah in the first four visions, except for a brief reference in 7.28, where 'the messiah' simply appears for a time and then dies, before the world reverts to primordial silence prior to the divine judgment and the renewal of paradise. In the fifth vision, the creature like a lion confronting the eagle which has brought such terror and grievous oppression over the world is interpreted as 'the Messiah . . . from the line of David' (IV Ezra 11.36–46; 12.10–39). The confrontation, however, is not military but forensic. His principal role is to 'denounce' the Romans 'before his judgment seat' – and then to deliver the remnant of the people (12.32–34). In the sixth vision, 'the man coming up out of the heart of the sea' is interpreted as God's 'son' who confronts the extensive forces arrayed against him. Again the figure is portrayed explicitly as not being a warrior. Rather, he 'reproves' and 'reproaches' the enemies and destroys them by means of the law (13.1–13, 25–39). Again in 14.9 'the messiah' is mentioned, but only incidentally. Although the interpretation of the fifth vision portrays the lion explicitly as 'the Messiah . . . of David', the interpretations of these figures also explicitly play down or even deny the military and monarchic features, concentrating instead on the judgmental role and that in the specific and limited matter of ending Roman imperial rule which had been so oppressive and destructive for Palestinian Jews.

For all its similarities with IV Ezra in provenance, form, and focal concern, the apocalypse of II Baruch has a significantly different portrayal of 'My Anointed One'. The first appearance, in chs. 29–30, is simply that, an appearance with virtually no function. The visions which form the climax of the apocalypse, however, portray God's anointed as the eschatological judge who will convict the last ruler of the fourth kingdom, i.e., Rome, whose power is more destructive and evil than that of preceding empires, and then kill him (II Bar. 39–40). Similarly, he will summon the nations to judgment, spare those which had not oppressed Israel (some of whom had been subjected by Israel), but deliver up to the sword those nations which had oppressed Israel, after which joy, rest, and other features of a new paradise will prevail (II Bar. 70–73). The Anointed One of II Baruch is not a military leader. In II Bar. 39.7 he replaces the 'humanlike one' of Daniel 7 as the recipient of sovereignty. Once installed in office, he then exercises the judgment of oppressive rulers that had been God's own earlier apocalyptic literature, such as Daniel and I Enoch. (One suspects that the traditional Christian construct of Jewish expectations of 'the messiah' must have been heavily dependent on II Bar. 39–40, 70–72.)

This survey of scribal groups' hopes for a solution to the difficult circumstances of imperial domination or even repression in which they were caught indicates that the earliest and most persistent solution was God's own intervention to condemn the imperial rulers and restore the people, as in the early Enoch literature and the visions of Daniel. In the later Similitudes of Enoch, perhaps contemporary with Jesus, the judgment is taken over by 'the Elect One/the Humanlike One' reminiscent of 'the humanlike one' of Daniel 7 which was originally a symbol of the people to be liberated, not an agent of deliverance. If some of these groups knew traditions about an 'anointed one' and/or Davidic king, they did not focus on such a figure as the principal agent of redemption. The Dead Sea community, which focused on God's own action for deliverance, in three of its many writings referred to the time of fulfilment with a stereotyped phrase of 'the rise of the messiah of Aaron and Israel', which is likely to have represented the ideal leadership-and-structure of the present and future community patterned after the original second-temple ideal of anointed priest together with anointed Davidic prince. The community that produced the Psalms of Solomon is the only group that places an anointed son of David in the central redemptive role. Their *messiah*, however, is explicitly not a military leader, but is rather portrayed as a scribal figure using the word rather than the sword. The two apocalypses struggling to come to grips with the Roman devastation of Jerusalem and the temple, finally, have God place judgment in the hands of a transcendent 'anointed one' who in neither IV Ezra nor II Baruch is portrayed as a warrior, but who actually slays the oppressive Roman rulers after the judgment in II Baruch. There is clearly a wide variety both of schemes of future deliverance and, in those few scribal communities which mentioned some sort of 'messiah', of images of particular messiahs' roles. In all cases prior to the Roman destruction of the temple-state, however, these groups' hopes for deliverance focus on condemnation of Jewish high-priestly as well as foreign imperial rulers.

Popular 'Messianic' and 'Prophetic' Movements[9]

We have little evidence for what the vast majority of people in ancient Palestine were thnking or doing. Through occasional hostile reports by the Jewish historian Josephus, however, we have windows on to several popular movements that took distinctively Jewish forms, suggesting continuing influence of ancient biblical tradition of protest and deliverance.

Contrary to modern scholarly handbooks, there is virtually no literary evidence for Jewish expectations of some sort of 'eschatological prophet' or 'new Moses'. (Only for a returning Elijah are there a few literary references, such as Sirach 48.1–14.) Nevertheless, in mid-first-century Palestine there arose a number of popular prophets who organized movements reminiscent of the great prophet-heroes of ancient Israel. According to the disdainful Josephus:

> Impostors and demagogues, under the guise of divine inspiration, provoked revolutionary actions and impelled the masses to act like madmen. They led them out into the wilderness so that there God would show them signs of imminent liberation. (*Jewish War* 2.259)

> When Fadus was governor of Judaea, a charlatan named Theudas persuaded most of the common people to take their possessions and follow him to the Jordan river. He said he was a prophet, and that at his command the river would be divided and allow them an easy crossing . . . Fadus sent out the cavalry . . . and killed many in a surprise attack. (*Antiquities* 20.97–98).

> An Egyptian (Jew) arrived at Jerusalem, saying he was a prophet and advising the mass of the common people to go with him to the Mount of Olives, which is just opposite the city. . . . He said that from there he wanted to show them that at his command the walls of Jerusalem would fall down and they could then make an entry into the city. Felix (and) his soldiers killed four hundred of them and took two hundred alive (*Antiquities* 20.169–71).

It is not difficult to discern here movements led by prophets proceeding to realize fantasies of new deliverance patterned after God's great acts of liberation in Israel's formative history, such as the exodus through the waters into the wilderness led by Moses or the victorious battle of Jericho led by Joshua. Clearly memory of these great events of the past were determining the social form taken by these popular *prophetic* movements in the mid-first century CE. (And it seems clear that the same tradition of popular prophets like Moses, Joshua, or Elijah have influenced the shaping of the chains of miracle stories now appearing in Mark 4–8, and perhaps the *semeia* source behind John as well.)

Very different in social form were several other popular movements, or rather insurrections, led by men acclaimed by the followers as 'kings'. Immediately after the death of the oppressive tyrant Herod, in every major district of Palestine, there erupted one of these popular *messianic* movements.

> Judas, son of the brigand-chief Ezekias, when he had organized a large number of desperate men at Sepphoris in Galilee, raided the palace . . . made off with all the goods that had been seized there. He caused fear . . . in his pursuit of royal rank. (*Antiquities* 17.271–72)

> (In Peraea) Simon, spurred on by chaotic social conditions, dared to don the diadem. When he had organized some men, he was also proclaimed king by them in their fantaticism. . . . After setting fire to the royal palace in Jericho, he plundered and carried off the things that had previously been taken there. He also set fire to numerous other royal residences in many parts of the country. (*Antiquities* 17.273–75)

> (In Judaea) Athronges, an obscure shepherd, . . . aspired to the kingship. . . . He held power for a long time, having been designated king. . . . He slaughtered both the Romans and the Herodian troops . . . because of the outrages they committed during Herod's rule and because of the wrongs they had perpetrated. (*Antiquities* 17.278–82)

That is, the long-pent-up popular frustration over Roman and Herodian conquest and oppression burst forth not in random and chaotic violence, but in the distinctive social form of movements headed by leaders whom the followers recognized as 'kings'. These movements then directed their energies quite pointedly at the royal palaces and storehouses where the rulers had taken and stored goods taken from the people. It seems clear that, like the popular prophetic movements, the distinctive social form taken by these movements led by kings were also determined by long-standing historical memories: in this case of the movements led by the popularly 'anointed' kings Saul, Jehu, and particularly the young David. The same tradition of popular messianic movements emerged again in the middle of the Jewish Revolt against Rome of 66–70 CE, when Simon bar Giora built a movement in the Judaean countryside, proclaiming the release of captives, and, after entering Jerusalem, formed the most powerful fighting force against the Roman reconquest of Jerusalem. Then again in the second great revolt of 132–135 CE, when Rabbi Akiba (TJ Ta'anit 4.8) proclaimed Bar Kokhba to be 'the Star out of Jacob' of Balaam's oracle (viewed as a messianic prophecy, Num. 24.17), the insurrection apparently took the same distinctive social form of a popular messianic movement.

Unlike the scribal groups who simply fantasized and wrote about future deliverance through God's intervention or divine judgment exercised either by God or by a historical or transcendent anointed one or by a transcendent human-like one, the Jewish peasantry formed concrete movements of deliverance. These movements assumed two distinctively Jewish social forms, patterned respectively after the great acts of liberation in Israelite history, the movements of exodus and conquest led by the prophetic figures Moses and Joshua, or the insurrectionary movements of popular independence led by figures popularly anointed or acclaimed as 'kings'. It is not difficult to realize that these Jewish popular movements are of far greater relevance than the traditional synthetic Christian concept of 'the messiah' in our attempts to understand Jesus' ministry and the origins of certain Jesus movements behind the development of Synoptic Gospel traditions. The apocalyptic reflections and other images of a transcendent messiah or a transcendent humanlike figure, on the other hand, are pertinent to our attempts to evaluate the developing Christian speculation on Jesus' special significance as the decisive agent of deliverance for their communities of faith.

Notes

1. For a fuller sketch of the basic social structural conflict in ancient Palestine, see R. A. Horsley, *Sociology and the Jesus Movement*, New York 1989, chs. 4–5.

2. R. A. Horsley, *Jesus and the Spiral of Violence*, San Francisco 1987, ch. 1, is a general characterization of such a 'colonial' or 'imperial' situation.

3. For some exploratory probings into the mediating position and potential conflicts in which the scribal class were placed, see *Jesus and the Spiral of Violence*, 129–46.

4. On the difference between official ideology of kingship and popular kingship, see R. A. Horsley, 'Popular Messianic Movements Around the Time of Jesus', *CBQ* 46, 1984, 473–8.

5. See the discerning discussion of the ideology of the high priesthood in B. L. Mack, *Wisdom and Hebrew Epic: Ben Sira's Hymn in Praise of the Fathers*, Chicago 1985.

6. On I Enoch, see G. W. E. Nickelsburg, 'Salvation without and with a Messiah:

Developing Beliefs in Writings Ascribed to Enoch', in J. Neusner *et al.* (ed.), *Judaisms and Their Messiahs at the Turn of the Christian Era*, Cambridge 1987, 49–68.

7. On Daniel, see esp. J. J. Collins, *The Apocalyptic Imagination*, New York 1984, ch. 3.

8. On IV Ezra, see M. E. Stone, 'The Question of the Messiah in IV Ezra', in *Judaisms and their Messiahs*, 209–24.

9. Further discussion of these popular movements in R. A. Horsley, 'Popular Messianic Movements around the Time of Jesus', *CBQ* 46, 1984, 471–95; '"Like One of the Prophets of Old": Two Types of Popular Prophets at the Time of Jesus', *CBQ* 47, 1985; and *Bandits, Prophets, and Messiahs: Popular Movements at the Time of Jesus* (with J. S. Hanson), San Francisco 1985, chs 3–4.

The Early Christians and Jewish Messianic Ideas

Seán Freyne

Even a cursory perusal of the literature of second-temple Judaism indicates that the notion of the Messiah had a quite complex history, and that contrary to popular Christian perceptions, it had no univocal meaning among the varieties of often-competing Judaisms that we can document from the literary remains of the period. This very generalized observation should alert us to the danger of reading into our early Christian sources, and by implication into Israelite and Jewish ones as well, ideas about the Messiah whose provenance is not from within Judaism, and which have little to do with the ways in which that figure is depicted in the literature of the second temple period.[1] As is well known, early Christian literature is itself a diverse and varied collection of responses to different life-situations. It should not surprise us, therefore, to find that even within the confines of this restricted body of writing a variety of uses and understandings of the Messiah-idea were operative and functioned in quite different ways, especially in view of the acrimonious debates that existed between the Jesus followers and other branches of Judaism in the period. Indeed, one might suspect that a group which, at a relatively early stage of its life, had named itself from a derivative of the Greek version of the Hebrew word Messiah, would be likely to have appropriated the idea in a highly distinctive, not to say polemical, manner as part of its own self-defining process.

This preliminary statement of the topic to be explored in this article would seem to ignore one vital aspect of the question, namely that Jesus had, himself, appropriated the title Messiah, and in such a highly distinctive manner, it is claimed, that he utterly transformed it. Thus, the foundations are laid for the early Christian christological reflections in the 'implicit christology' of the earthly Jesus' life and career. Implied in claims such as this is the assumption that christology is a direct and unilinear development from Jewish messianic aspirations and expressions. Yet this assumption ignores the fact that a very different thought-world had entered the picture once the Jesus movement came into contact with Greek ideas and conceptions – something that we can attribute in the first instance to those Hellenists from Cyprus and Cyrene who at Antioch 'spoke to the Greeks also, preaching the Lord Jesus' (Acts 11.20). One aspect of that thought-world that was to play a very significant role in the development of later christology (as distinct from Jewish messianism, with due respect to the over-simplification of such a phrase) was the understanding that saviours and hero-figures who intervened in the affairs of humans shared in some way in the being of the divine that they represented, and were not just chosen or anointed for a mission. The dominant philosophical trend as evidenced for example in Philo, the Jewish Platonist philosopher from Alexandria, had shown how Jewish religious beliefs in this regard could be transformed through translation into philosophical categories dealing specifically with the divine action and presence in the world.[2] In the light of this consideration our starting point must be, not the historical Jesus and his real or alleged claims to messianic status during his lifetime – though we shall return to this question at the end – but the texts which the early Christians produced and which witness to this interfacing and trans-forming of one tradition by the other in a variety of social and religious settings. As we re-read the various accounts our focus, therefore, will be on the extent, if any, to which more traditional Jewish understandings of the Messiah and his role/s) play in early Christianity's development of its own claims.

The Messiah in early Christian letters

The procedure of following a chronological approach by starting with the Pauline epistle should not obscure the fact that the Gospels may retain older strands of Christian usage, though now embedded in later writings. One might have expected that Paul's letters would reflect the Jewish attitudes to the Messiah, in view of their dates and the undoubted Jewish affiliations of their author. Yet in the opinion of most commentators the vast number of the 379 occurrences of the word *christos* in the Pauline letters designates a proper name and is not used for the role to be played by some awaited figure(s), as is the case in other near-contemporary Jewish writings.[3] True, Paul does seem to refer to this more general Jewish expectation at the outset of his theological apologia for Jewish unbelief: 'From them is the Christ according to the flesh'; yet even in this context it is distinguished from the distinctly Christian understanding: 'I wish to be cut off from Christ for the sake of my kinsmen' (Rom. 9.3.6). The phrase 'according to the flesh', recalling its opposite 'according to the Spirit', is used here, not to point to Jesus' earthly origins (as in Rom. 1.2–4), but to distinguish between the Jewish understanding of the Messiah (which could be counted as one of the blessings of that heritage along with other pillars of Jewish religious self-identity) and the distinctly Christian, not to say Pauline usage of the name as an inclusive designation of all those who came to believe in Jesus, thereby constituting 'the body of Christ'.

When one turns to the post-Pauline letters and the other New Testament epistles (irrespective of the dating of these writings), there seems to be an equally mystifying lack of interest in current ideas or images associated with the Messiah, as known to us from Jewish writings. This absence of any sustained discussion of other prevailing views – and these were many and varied – about the Messiah might be interpreted as Paul's and others' recognition of the lack of interest in or knowledge of such issues among the largely Gentile communities. Yet, in Paul's case, at least, this answer is scarcely adequate in itself, in view of his creative appropriation of other aspects of the Jewish heritage to develop his theological ideas, even when these were not likely to have been familiar to his presumed readership. He is aware that the Christ he proclaims, namely a crucified one, is a scandal to the Jews (I Cor. 1.23). Elsewhere he writes that there are some that want to pervert 'the gospel of Christ' by another gospel, the existence of which Paul vehemently denies, and he condemns those who would preach 'another Jesus' (Gal. 1.7; II Cor. 11.4). For Paul, it would seem, the title Christ has been defined by the career of Jesus, especially his death, and he is not particularly concerned to justify this appropriation of the title in terms of other Jewish expressions or expectations.

As a proper name Christ Jesus (or Jesus Christ) had an authoritative ring, especially when the further title *kyrios* or Lord is added, even for those who had no knowledge of the specific background of *Christos* within the Jewish messianic thought-world. It would have sounded like 'Imperator Caesar' to those who were accustomed to having honorific epithets added to proper names. For Paul, however, the distinctive theological significance of the name was based on the fact that it was the proper name of the one who had been crucified and raised with redemptive consequences, in his belief, for the whole human family. The body/person of the

Risen Christ was for him the symbol of restored humanity in which all were invited to participate. Jewish tradition was familiar with the idea of individuals who were representative of the whole group – Abraham, Jacob (Israel) and above all Adam – and it was this line of thought rather than messianic hopes that inspired Paul to identify Christ as the new Adam, even if the blessings associated with Christ were also part of the general messianic picture: peace, justice, reconciliation (see Rom. 5.12–19).

Paul thereby bypassed the distinctively nationalistic associations of the messianic idea and moved instead in another, cosmic sphere that was based on the apocalyptic understanding of God's triumph over evil and the emergence of the new age.[4] While other first-century Jewish writings ascribe a role to the Messiah in the unfolding of the end-time, apocalyptic drama, Paul does not develop the role of Jesus in this way, with the possible exception of I Cor. 15.23–28 (Syrian Baruch 29.3–30.1; 39.7; 73.1; 74.2; IV Esdras 7.26–29).[5] For the most part, however, it is the triumph of God, manifested in the death and resurrection of Jesus, that provides the controlling metaphor for his thinking. Avoidance of the politico-nationalistic aspects of the image may have played some role in the context of a Gentile mission outside Palestine, but it was the need to develop an inclusive theological framework for that highly successful mission that prompted the development of his thought in Romans, the most complete statement of his position. In terms of our present discussion it is noteworthy that when he does come to develop his hopes for Israel's future within that context (Rom. 9–11), he does not draw on the messianic ideal or base an argument on the messianic status of Jesus, but pins his hopes rather on the final plan or *mysterion* of God for history that has begun to unfold in the career of Jesus.

Early Christian narratives and the Messiah

The issue of the messiahship of Jesus is central to all the Gospels, even though it is possible to detect quite distinctive emphases in each, related to their specific audiences and situations.

Mark's is the earliest extant narrative, and there we encounter the mysterious nature of the claims to Jesus' messiahship within the community to which the Gospel is addressed. The issue of a correct identification is vital, since there is an explicit warning against false Christs and false prophets, 'deceiving if possible, even the elect' (Mark 13.22) in the context of the apocalyptic discourse that has the Jewish War of 66–70 in its sights. Whether we are to assume a Roman readership in the wake of

Nero's persecution or a Palestinian one on the eve of a Roman onslaught on Jerusalem, the Markan community needs to be clear on the precise sense in which it is prepared to confess Jesus as the Messiah.[6] The passion story centred upon the charge of claiming to be 'king of the Jews' indicates the strongly political overtones that messianic claims could carry and the consequences accruing to anyone claiming such a status. But Jesus' messiahship, as the Markan readers and others interested in knowing are assured, is not of that order. At the pivotal moment of the Gospel when Peter proclaims him as the Christ, the reader is alerted that all is not well with such a bald proclamation, since Jesus immediately enjoins silence on the disciples in tones reminiscent of other instances within the narrative where an erroneous interpretation of his identity was likely (8.30; see 1.44; 3.12; 5.43; 7.36). Furthermore, as if to distance himself from Peter's identification, Jesus immediately instructs the disciples that the Son of Man (and not the lately confessed Messiah) must suffer and be rejected. This instruction is repeated twice subsequently, yet as the group approaches Jerusalem, James and John continue to misunderstand, requesting special places in the kingdom.

By inference, therefore, Mark fills in for us some of the missing links in Paul's apparent ignoring of the wider Jewish messianic expectations. The followers of Jesus should be clear on the meaning of Jesus' messiahship. A genuine understanding of the claim did not include the usual political implications which were standard in other popular Jewish messianic pretenders of the period. Thus, Roman imperial power, rather than the theological demands of a universal mission, lies behind this particular portrayal. Yet it also points backwards to Jesus' career, and suggests a hesitancy about his own position on the matter. We shall return to this point later.

Matthew's and Luke's Gospels both reflect the post-70 situation and the fall of Jerusalem in particular. This momentous event in terms of the ancient world generally, alluded to by Tacitus, the Roman historian, has left its imprint on the understanding of Jesus' messiahship in these two Gospels in quite distinctive ways. In Matthew we sense an aggressive messianization of the whole career of Jesus, supported by a proof-text technique which claims fulfilment of the Hebrew scriptures in the career of Jesus. Jesus was Son of David, even when Matthew wants to say more than that about him as Emmanuel, 'God with us'. As Son of David he is 'the one who is called the Christ' (1.17), a claim that even Pilate voices to the Jewish authorities at the trial (27.17.22). Both the works and teaching of Jesus take on an explicit messianic status (Matt. 11.2; 23.10). His coming from

Galilee does not disqualify him from the role of Messiah, since that too was divinely planned and echoed God's activity in and to Israel.[7]

This picture has to be set in the wider context of the claims that Matthew is seeking to establish over against other versions, of where the true Israel is to be found and how it is to be constituted. In Matthew's view all other versions of Judaism have lost the right to claim to be the people of God, because they have rejected those sent to them by God – the prophets, Jesus and those whom he sent to them (Matt. 21.43; 22.1–14; 23.34–36). The climax of this rejection has been God's rejection of Jerusalem and those who claimed legitimation for their religious views from that centre. Therefore, Jesus is the only legitimate claimant to messianic status. In the final confrontation between Jesus and the Pharisees in the Gospel, the question arises of identifying the Messiah in terms of whose son he is. The biblical proof-text (Ps. 110.1) implies that the Messiah is more than David's son, since he addresses him as Lord, a title which Matthew consistently applies to Jesus throughout the Gospel. The narrator informs us that from that day forward no one dared to ask him any more questions, since, it is implied, Jesus has established himself as the definitive interpreter of scripture, the true messianic teacher of Israel.

Luke is equally interested in identifying Jesus as the Messiah of Israel. From the outset of the narrative the child who is born is linked to the city of David: he will receive the throne of David his father; the angels announce to the shepherds that in the city of David a Saviour has been born who is Christ, the Lord; Anna and Simeon are represented as looking for 'the redemption of Jerusalem' and 'the consolation of Israel', as they enthusiastically receive the child in the temple (Luke 1.32; 2.11, 25, 38). This identification of Jesus as the Messiah of Israel is repeated throughout the Acts of the Apostles, Luke's second volume, in the context of early Christian missionary proclamation. This preoccupation is all the more striking in view of the fact that, as we have seen, it was not a concern for Paul in the same way, who simply took over the name *Christos* but did not develop its theological implications directly from a Jewish messianic perspective.

The proclamation of Jesus in the synagogue at Nazareth provides the interpretative framework for the presentation of his messianic career. In the citation from Isaiah that is there put on the lips of Jesus, the verbal form, 'to anoint' (*echrisen*), rather than the name *Christos* is used, suggesting a more dynamic understanding of the role in terms of the stipulations of the jubilee year, with the remission of debts and the release of captives. Equally in Acts Jesus is said to have been anointed with the

Holy Spirit and with power and to have gone around 'doing good, because God was with him' (Acts 10.37). Thus, for Luke the role of the Messiah is considerably broadened to include the general prophetic call for justice, even when that demand was itself inspired by the hopes for an ideal Israel associated with the arrival of the Messiah. Nevertheless, Luke's broadening of the Messiah's role to that of prophet of justice was inspired by the social circumstances of his own community, comprising of rich and poor. It was that social setting rather than any particular Jewish depiction of that role that shaped his particular presentation of the career of Jesus as messianic.[8]

In one respect Luke does seem to be addressing other Jews directly in his treatment of Jesus as Messiah. 'Was it not necessary that the Christ should suffer these things and enter into his glory?' is the pointed question put to two disciples on the road to Emmaus, mourning the death of Jesus as the one whom they hoped to deliver Israel (Luke 24.21, 26). The idea of a suffering Messiah is found in 'all the scriptures', something that is echoed at the outset of Acts (3.18). It is Paul, however, as depicted by Luke, who develops this theme most consistently in the latter part of the narrative. At Thessalonica he argued from the scriptures, explaining that it was necessary for Christ to suffer, and that the Jesus whom he proclaimed was the Christ (Acts 17.2f.). Later a message in very similar tones was delivered in front of Agrippa (Acts 26.22f.). It is tempting to see the defence of this aspect of Jesus' career in the context of actual disputes with Jews in the Diaspora synagogues, since in each city that he visits, Paul is repeatedly portrayed as entering the Jewish synagogue first, only to be rejected, thereby prompting his turning to the Gentiles. We seem to be faced with the paradoxical situation that the further removed the narrative is from the actual historical situation, the more the messiahship of Jesus has to be defended by early Christian writers.

This becomes particularly apparent in the Fourth Gosepl, where the question of the origins, identity and role of the Messiah seem to be crucial to the account.[9] Unlike Matthew and Luke, however, this is with a view not to validating the claims about Jesus, but rather to acting as a foil against which those claims are developed and refined. It is in this work above all that we can see the process, mentioned earlier, at work, namely the wedding of traditional Jewish expectations with the transcendentalism of the Greco-Roman philosophical milieu as applied to Jesus' career.

Two distinct lines of messianic expectation are depicted in the work. On the one hand, there are the expectations of the first disciples whose views are affirmed, while a further and greater insight is promised to them (John

1.19–51). In addition there are the views of the opponents who have equally strong ideas about the Messiah and see these as disqualifying the claims of Jesus. Each group must be examined briefly.

The meeting between Jesus and his first disciples takes place in the context of a discussion between John the Baptist and the Jewish authorities as to whether John himself might be the Messiah.[10] He denies this, pointing instead to Jesus whom he confesses as Lamb of God and Son of God. Not surprisingly then, the first disciples came from John to Jesus, acknowledging him in traditional Jewish categories: the Messiah (1.41 – the only use of the Hebrew word in the New Testament which is then translated by the Greek *Christos*), 'the one about whom Moses in the law and all the prophets wrote' (v. 45); 'the Son of God, the King of Israel' (v. 49). This scene is bracketed by two explicit statements about the heavenly origins of Jesus. The closing verses of the prologue (addressed to the reader) identify Jesus Christ as the one who is 'full of grace and truth' and who alone can make God known (1.17f.), and by way of conclusion Nathanael (and by implication, all who share his openness) is promised greater things still in terms of a vision that will identify Jesus as the heavenly Son of Man in whom the divine presence dwells (1.50f.). As the revelatory discourses unfold, the disciples do indeed see his glory and believe in him (2.11; 6.68; 11.15), not just in Jewish messianic terms, but in distinctively Johannine categories, of which the two statements just mentioned are examples.

Others, however, mainly categorized as 'the Jews', fail to recognize him for various reasons, mainly connected with their preconceptions about the Messiah. Their belief, based on scripture, is that the Messiah's origins will not be known (7.27.41f.), and he will remain for ever (12.34f.). This information clearly disqualifies Jesus in the opponents' views (see 6.42). There is no agreement among commentators as to which, if any, circles of Judaism these alleged beliefs about the Messiah belong. What is important for the argument of the Gospel is that those who judge Jesus' claims by these rigid criteria are grievously mistaken. There is comic irony in the fact that for the author and the ideal reader Jesus' true origins with God are known, and that he does remain with God for ever as the exalted one of their beliefs. The author's and the opponents' views of the Messiah are diametrically opposed, and so anyone who confesses Jesus as the Christ was to be expelled from the synagogue (9.22).

There are, then, two competing views about the Messiah in the Fourth Gospel. The quite traditional understanding of the disciples was capable of being transformed into full-blown Johannine christology by juxtaposing the traditional titles with distinctive Johannine terms such as Logos and (heavenly) Son of Man, as well as with a variety of symbolic designations: light, life, bread, shepherd, vine – many of which had been used in the Hebrew scriptures for God. This presentation corresponds to the Johannine treatment of faith as a progressive process from initial encounter to depth experience, something that is dramatically portrayed in various episodes such as the meeting of Jesus with the Samaritan woman (ch. 4) and the opening of the eyes of the man born blind (ch. 9). There is nothing inevitable about the progression, however. In the wake of the feeding miracle the crowd, perceiving that Jesus was a prophet, wanted to take him by force and make him king, but Jesus escaped from them, since from the point of view of the author the crowd's understanding was flawed, even though both titles can be used subsequently to fit the Johannine understanding of Jesus as revealer of the truth (John 18.36–38).[11] Indeed the purpose of the work as a whole is to generate faith in Jesus as the Christ and Son of God, but only when these are understood in a thoroughly Johannine fashion that can lead to life as defined by the Johannine Jesus (20.30f; see 11.25–27). Equally, rigid expectations about the Messiah which attempt to impose pre-determined criteria of identification are for the author of the Gospel symptomatic of the mentality that makes Johannine faith impossible, in that they exclude any sense of searching, openness to new experiences or recognition of the need to reinterpret one's previous assumptions in the light of a changed situation.

In all of this one cannot mistake the polemical situation that existed between the Johannine community and the synagogue, something that many recent studies of the Gospel have underlined.[12] The notion of the Messiah had clearly become an issue on both sides. For 'the Jews', belief in Jesus as the Messiah merited the ultimate sanction of expulsion and even persecution, whereas for the Johannine Christians such a belief could, and presumably in the case of its earliest members, did, form the starting point for their subsequent understanding of Jesus' person and role. By the time the Gospel came to be written, the political implications of the Messiah's role were no longer of any significance, since both Jesus and Pilate had repudiated any implications of a threat to Rome. The question of the Messiah was now a theological matter in the strict sense, something that would divide Jews and Christians down to our own time.

Conclusion

This survey of early Christian literature in its two broadest generic forms – letters and Gospels – has revealed quite a surprising conclusion as far as the figure of the Messiah is concerned, at least in terms of popular Christian perceptions. From being an accepted proper name for Jesus in the Pauline communities it became an increasingly polemical issue the further the move from the actual career of Jesus. Its problematic character first surfaces in our texts in Mark's Gospel, where the perceived threat to Rome's imperial power had to be answered reassuringly for all concerned through the figure of a crucified rather than a politically active Messiah.[13] Subsequently, it became a central issue of theological definition and polemics between competing Jewish and Christian orthodoxies.

There are many unanswered questions, not least that of when and by whom Jesus was first categorized in this way. Though the Gospels clearly reflect the situations current at their time of writing, they can still properly be questioned concerning the situation during the career of the earthly Jesus, provided due caution is used.[14] A ministry such as that attributed to Jesus in the Gospels, even in its broad outlines, would inevitably have raised the question of how to categorize this person, even by those opposed to the whole thrust of his words and works. Both Mark and John hint at popular stirrings that can be broadly described as messianic, and the disappointment among his close followers further suggests that the question of the messianic status of Jesus had been raised during his own lifetime. Once Jesus was unwilling to accept a narrowly political role, avoidance of any personal claims in favour of the more general kingly rule of God would appear to have been his strategy, and even then his parabolic utterances about the nature of that reign underline the dangerous and delicate hermeneutical enterprise on which he was engaged.[15]

Faced with the scandal and disappointment of his death, it would appear that the need for the first followers to interpret their experience of God's triumph in the face of apparent failure lead to an aggressive appropriation of various symbolic expressions from the Hebrew scriptures about the ultimate vindication of God's plan, not least those relating to the royal Davidic line.[16] Thus began the process of a distinctly Christian understanding of the Messiah and his role, a process that reached its climax in the Fourth Gospel's theological utterances that transformed Jewish messianic hopes into Christian christological claims.

In the light of this account it would seem that the issue of the messianic status of Jesus need not continue to be the stumbling block it has been in Jewish-Christian relations down to the present day. If Jesus himself was reluctant to accept the epithet in order to avoid any misunderstanding of the nature of God's kingly rule that he felt called on to proclaim and live out, then those who seek to be true to his vision need have little compunction in leaving to God's future the final determination of his status in the divine plan for human history. Such modesty would not be unfaithful to the eschatological direction of the texts which Christians hold as sacred, notwithstanding the usefulness of messianic symbolism for exploring and defining early Christian self-understanding and life-style, which those very texts so clearly demonstrate.

Notes

1. See the important collection of essays, *Judaisms and Their Messiahs at the Turn of the Christian Era*, ed. J. Neusner, W. Scott Green and E. Frerichs, Cambridge 1987.

2. See John M. Dillon, 'Logos and Trinity: Patterns of Platonist Influence on Early Christianity', in *The Philosophy in Christianity*, ed. G. Vesey, Cambridge 1989, 1–13.

3. See W. Grundmann, '*Christos* in Paul's Epistles', *Theological Dictionary of the New Testament*, ed. G. Kittel and G. Friedrich, IX, Grand Rapids 1974, 540ff.

4. See J. C. Beker, *Paul the Apostle. The Triumph of God in Life and Thought*, Philadelphia 1980.

5. M. Stone, 'The Question of the Messiah in 4 Ezra', in *Judaisms and Their Messiahs* (n.1), 209–25.

6. For recent proposals on the situation of Mark see C. Myers, *Binding the Strong Man*, Maryknoll 1990; B. Mack, *A Myth of Innocence. Mark and Christian Origins*, Philadelphia 1988.

7. See D. Harrington, 'Jesus, the Son of David, the Son of Abraham . . . Christology and Second Temple Judaism', *Irish Theological Quarterly* 57, 1991, 184–95.

8. See H. Moxnes, *The Economy of the Kingdom. Social Conflict and Economic Relations in Luke's Gospel*, Philadelphia 1988.

9. M. de Jonge, 'Jewish Expectations about the Messiah according to the Fourth Gospel', *New Testament Studies* 19, 1973, 246–70.

10. See J. Ashton, *Understanding the Fourth Gospel*, Oxford 1991, 238–91.

11. W. Meeks, *The Prophet-King-Moses Traditions in the Fourth Gospel*, Leiden 1967.

12. The studies of J. L. Martyn have been pioneering in this respect. See his *History and Theology in the Fourth Gospel*, New York 1963.

13. See R. Horsley, 'Popular Messianic Movements around the Time of Jesus', *Catholic Biblical Quarterly* 46, 1984, 471–95, for an account of the actual political situation that would have determined the way in which Jesus was likely to have been perceived in Roman eyes.

14. See my *Galilee, Jesus and the Gospels. Literary Approaches and Historical Investigations*, Dublin 1988.

15. The thesis proposed by S. G. F. Brandon that Jesus was the leader of a Zealot band, a role that has now been suppressed in the Gospels, has been discredited. See

M. Hengel, *Was Jesus a Revolutionist?*, Philadelphia 1971, for some telling counter-arguments.

16. See N. Dahl, 'The Crucified Messiah', in *The Crucified Messiah and Other Essays*, Minneapolis 1974, 23–38.

II · Historical

When did Judaism become a Messianic Religion?

Jacob Neusner

Within the Judaism born in the centuries after 70, the distinct traditions of priest, sage, and messianist were joined in a new way. In the person of the rabbi, holy man, Torah incarnate, avatar and model of the son of David, rabbinic Judaism found its sole overarching system. So the diverse varieties of Judaic piety present in Israel before 70 came to be bonded over the next several centuries in a wholly unprecedented way, with each party to the union imposing its logic upon the other constituents of the whole. The ancient categories remained. But they were so profoundly revised and transformed that nothing was preserved intact. Judaism as we know it, the Judaism of Scripture and Mishnah, Midrash (from the second to the sixth century CE) and Talmud, thereby effected the ultimate transvaluation of all the values, of all the kinds of Judaism that had come before, from ancient Israel onward. Through the person and figure of the rabbi, the whole burden of Israel's heritage was taken up, renewed and handed on from late antiquity to the present day. At issue here is: at what point in the formation of the Judaism represented by the canonical documents, Mishnah, Talmuds, Midrash, did the Messiah-theme assume prominence?[1]

The character of the Israelite scriptures, with their emphasis upon historical narrative as a mode of theological explanation, leads us to expect all Judaisms to evolve as deeply messianic religions. With all prescribed actions pointed toward the coming of the Messiah at the end of time, and all interest focused upon answering the historical-salvific questions ('how long?'), Judaism from late antiquity to the present day presents no surprises. Its liturgy evokes historical events to prefigure salvation;

prayers of petition repeatedly turn to the speedy coming of the Messiah; and the experience of worship invariably leaves the devotee expectant and hopeful. Just as rabbinic Judaism is a deeply messianic religion, secular extensions of Judaism have commonly proposed secularized versions of the focus upon history and have shown interest in the purpose and dénouement of events. Teleology again appears as an eschatology embodied in messianic symbols.

Yet, for a brief moment, a vast and influential document presented a kind of Judaism in which history did not define the main framework by which the issue of teleology took a form other than the familiar eschatological one and in which historical events were absorbed, through their trivialization in taxonomic structures, into an ahistorical system. In the kind of Judaism in this document, messiahs played a part. But these 'anointed men' had no historical role. They undertook a task quite different from that assigned to Jesus by the framers of the Gospels. They were merely a species of priest, falling into one classification rather than another. That document is the Mishnah, a strange corpus of normative statements which we may, though with some difficulty, classify as a law code or a school book for philosophical jurists. By c.600 CE a system of Judaism emerged in which the Mishnah as foundation document would be asked to support a structure at best continuous with, but in no way fully defined by the outlines of, the Mishnah itself.

Coming at the system from the asymmetrical endpoint, we ask the Mishnah to answer the questions at hand. What of the Messiah? When will he come? To whom, in Israel, will he come? And what must, or can, we do while we wait to hasten his coming? If we now reframe these questions and divest them of their mythic cloak, we ask about the Mishnah's theory of the history and destiny of Israel and the purpose of the Mishnah's own system in relationship to Israel's present and end: the implicit teleology of the philosophical law at hand.

Answering these questions out of the resources of the Mishnah is not possible. The Mishnah presents no large view of history. It contains no reflection whatever on the nature and meaning of the destruction of the Temple in 70 CE, an event which surfaces only in connection with some changes in the law explained as resulting from the end of the cult. The Mishnah pays no attention to the matter of the end time. The word 'salvation' is rare, 'sanctification' commonplace. More strikingly, the framers of the Mishnah are virtually silent on the teleology of the system; they never tell us why we should do what the Mishnah tells us, let alone explain what will happen if we do. Incidents in the Mishnah are preserved either as narrative settings for the statement of the law, or, occasionally, as precedents. Historical events are classified and turned into entries on lists. But incidents in any case come few and far between. True, events do make an impact. But it always is for the Mishnah's own purpose and within its own taxonomic system and rule-seeking mode of thought. To be sure, the framers of the Mishnah may also have had a theory of the Messiah and of the meaning of Israel's history and destiny. But they kept it hidden, and their document manages to provide an immense account of Israel's life without explicitly telling us about such matters.

The Messiah in the Mishnah does not stand at the forefront of the framers' consciousness. The issues encapsulated in the myth and person of the Messiah are scarcely addressed. The framers of the Mishnah do not resort to speculation about the Messiah as a historical-supernatural figure. So far as that kind of speculation provides the vehicle for reflection on salvific issues, or in mythic terms, narratives on the meaning of history and the destiny of Israel, we cannot say that the Mishnah's philosophers take up those encompassing categories of being: Where are we heading? What can we do about it? That does not mean that questions found urgent in the aftermath of the destruction of the temple and the disaster of Bar Kokhba failed to attract the attention of the Mishnah's sages. But they treated history in a different way, offering their own answers to its questions. To these we now turn.

By 'history' I mean not merely events, but how events serve to teach lessons, reveal patterns, tell us what we must do and what will happen to us tomorrow. In that context, some events contain richer lessons than others: the destruction of the temple of Jerusalem teaches more than a crop failure, being kidnapped into slavery more than stubbing one's toe. Furthermore, lessons taught by events – 'history' in the didactic sense – follow a progression from trivial and private to consequential and public. The framers of the Mishnah explicitly refer to very few events, treating those they do mention with a focus quite separate from the unfolding events themselves. They rarely create narratives; historical events do not supply organizing categories or taxonomic classifications. We find no tractate devoted to the destruction of the temple, no complete chapter detailing the events of Bar Kokhba nor even a sustained celebration of the events of the sages' own historical lives. When things that have happened are mentioned, it is neither to narrate nor to interpret and draw lessons from the events. It is either to illustrate a point of law or to pose a problem of the law – always *en passant*, never in a pointed way.

The Mishnah absorbs into its encompassing system all events, small and large. With them the sages accomplish what they accomplish in everything else: a vast labour of taxonomy, an immense contruction of the order and rules governing the classification of everything on earth and in heaven. The disruptive character of history – one-time events of ineluctable significance – scarcely impresses the philosophers. They find no difficulty in showing that what appears unique and beyond classification has in fact happened before and so falls within the range of trustworthy rules and known procedures. Once history's components, one-time events, lose their distinctiveness, then history as a didactic intellectual construct, as a source of lessons and rules, also loses all pertinence.

So lessons and rules come from sorting things out and classifying them from the procedures and modes of thought of the philosopher seeking regularity. To this labour of taxonomy, the historian's way of selecting data and arranging them into patterns of meaning to teach lessons proves inconsequential. One-time events are not important. The world is composed of nature and supernature. The laws that count are those to be discovered in heaven and, in heaven's creation and counterpart, on earth. Keep those laws and things will work out. Break them, and the result is predictable: calamity of whatever sort will supervene in accordance with the rules. But just because it is predictable, a catastrophic happening testifies to what has always been and must always be, in accordance with reliable rules and within categories already discovered and well explained. That is why the lawyer-philosophers of the mid-second century produced the Mishnah – to explain how things are. Within the framework of well-classified rules, there could be messiahs, but no single Messiah.

If the end of time and the coming of the Messiah do not serve to explain, for the Mishnah's system, why people should do what the Mishnah says, then what alternative teleology does the Mishnah's first apologetic, Abot, provide? Only when we appreciate the clear answers given in that document, brought to closure at c.250, shall we grasp how remarkable is the shift which took place in later documents of the rabbinic canon, to a messianic framing of the issues of the Torah's ultimate purpose and value. Let us see how the framers of Abot, in the aftermath of the creation of the Mishnah, explain the purpose and goal of the Mishnah: an ahistorical, non-messianic teleology.

The first document generated by the Mishnah's heirs took up the work of completing the Mishnah's system by answering questions of purpose and meaning. Whatever teleology the Mishnah as such would ever acquire would derive from Abot, a collection of sayings by authorities who flourished in the generation after Judah the Patriarch; in all likelihood the document is of the mid-third-century rabbinic estate of the Land of Israel. Abot presents statements to express the ethos and ethic of the Mishnah, and so provides a kind of theory.

Abot agreed with the other sixty-two tractates: history proved no more important here than it had been before. With scarcely a word about history and no account of events at all, Abot manages to provide an ample account of how the Torah – written and oral, thus in later eyes, Scripture and Mishnah – came down to its own day. Accordingly, the passage of time as such plays no role in the explanation of the origins of the document, nor is the Mishnah presented as eschatological. Occurrences of great weight ('history') are never invoked. How then does the tractate tell the story of Torah, narrate the history of God's revelation to Israel, encompassing both Scripture and Mishnah? The answer is that Abot's framers manage to do their work of explanation without telling a story or invoking history at all. They pursue a different way of answering the same question, by exploiting a non-historical mode of thought and method of legitimation. And that is the main point: teleology serves the purpose of legitimation, and hence is accomplished in ways other than explaining how things originated or assuming that historical fact explains anything.

Disorderly historical events entered the system of the Mishnah and found their place within the larger framework of the Mishnah's orderly world. But to claim that the Mishnah's framers merely ignored what was happening would be incorrect. They worked out their own way of dealing with historical events, the disruptive power of which they not only conceded but freely recognized. Further, the Mishnah's authors did not intend to compose a history book or a work of prophecy or apocalypse. Even if they had wanted to narrate the course of events, they could hardly have done so through the medium of the Mishnah. Yet the Mishnah presents its philosophy in full awareness of the issues of historical calamity confronting the Jewish nation. So far as the philosophy of the document confronts the totality of Israel's existence, the Mishnah by definition also presents a philosophy of history.

The Mishnah's subordination of historical events contradicts the emphasis of a thousand years of Israelite thought. The biblical histories, the ancient prophets, the apocalyptic visionaries all had testified that events themselves were important. Events carried the message of the living God. Events constituted history, pointed towards, and so explained, Israel's destiny. An essentially ahistorical system of timeless sanctification, worked out through construction of an eternal rhythm which centred on the movement of the moon and stars and seasons, represented a life chosen by few outside the priesthood. Furthermore, the pretence that what happens matters less than what is, testified against palpable and memorable reality. Israel had suffered enormous loss of life. The Talmud of the Land of Israel takes these events seriously and treats them as unique and remarkable. The memories proved real. The hopes evoked by the Mishnah's promise of sanctification of a world in static perfection did not. For they had to compete with the grief of an entire century of mourning.

The most important change is the shift in historical thinking adumbrated in the pages of the Talmud of the Land of Israel, a shift from focus upon the temple and its supernatural history to close attention to the people Israel and its natural, this-worldly history. Once Israel, holy Israel, had come to form the counterpart to the temple and its supernatural life, that other history – Israel's – would stand at the centre of things. Accordingly, a new sort of memorable event came to the fore in the Talmud of the Land of Israel. Let me give this new history appropriate emphasis: it was the story of Israel's suffering, remembrance of that suffering, on the one side, and an effort to explain events of such tragedy, on the other. So a composite 'history' constructed out of the Yerushalmi's units of discourse which were pertinent to consequential events would contain long chapters on what happened to Israel, the Jewish people, and not only, or mainly, what had earlier occurred in the temple.

The components of the historical theory of Israel's sufferings were manifold. First and foremost, history taught moral lessons. Historical events entered into the construction of a teleology for the Yerushalmi's system of Judaism as a whole. What the law demanded reflected the consequences of wrongful action on the part of Israel. So, again, Israel's own deeds defined the events of history. Rome's role, like Assyria's and Babylonia's, depended upon Israel's provoking divine wrath as it was executed by the great empire. This mode of thought comes to simple expression in what follows.

Y. Erubin 3.9

[IV B]   R. Ba, R. Hiyya in the name of R. Yohanan: "'Do not gaze at me because I am swarthy, because the sun has scorched me. My mother's sons were angry with me, they made me keeper of the vineyards; but, my own vineyard, I have not kept!' [Song 1.6]. What made me guard the vineyards? It is because of not keeping my own vineyard.

[C]   What made me keep two festival days in Syria? It is because I did not keep the proper festival day in the Holy Land.

[D]   I imagined that I would receive a reward for the two days, but I received a reward only for one of them.

[E]   Who made it necessary that I should have to separate two pieces of dough-offering from grain grown in Syria? It is because I did not separate a single piece of dough-offering in the Land of Israel.'

Israel had to learn the lesson of its history so as also to take command of its own destiny.

But this notion of determining one's own destiny should not be misunderstood. The framers of the Talmud of the Land of Israel were not telling the Jews to please God by doing commandments in order that they should thereby gain control of their own destiny. On the contrary, the paradox of the Yerushalmi's system lies in the fact that Israel can free itself of control by other nations only by humbly agreeing to accept God's rule. The nations – Rome, in the present instance – rest on one side of the balance, while God rests on the other. Israel must then choose between them. There is no such thing for Israel as freedom from both God and the nations, total autonomy and independence. There is only a choice of masters, a ruler on earth or a ruler in heaven.

With propositions such as these, the framers of the Mishnah will certainly have concurred. And why not? For the fundamental affirmations of the Mishnah about the centrality of Israel's perfection in stasis – sanctification – readily prove congruent to the attitudes at hand. Once the Messiah's coming had become dependent upon Israel's condition and not upon Israel's actions in historical time, then the Mishnah's system will have imposed its fundamental and definitive character upon the Messiah myth. An eschatological teleology framed through that myth then would prove wholly appropriate to the method of the larger system of the Mishnah. When this fact has been fully and completely spelled out, we shall then have grasped the distinctive history of the myth of the Messiah in the formative history of Judaism.

What, after all, makes a messiah a false messiah? In this Talmud, it is not his claim to save Israel, but his claim to save Israel without the help of God. The meaning of the true Messiah is Israel's total submission, through the Messiah's gentle rule, to God's yoke and service. So God is not to be manipulated through Israel's humouring of heaven in rite and cult. The notion of keeping the commandments so as to please heaven and get God to do what Israel wants is totally incongruent to the text at hand. Keeping the commandments as a mark of submission, loyalty, humility before God is the rabbinic system of salvation. So Israel does not 'save itself'. Israel never controls its own destiny, either on earth or in heaven. The only choice is whether to cast one's fate into the hands of cruel, deceitful men, or to trust in the living God of mercy and love. We shall now see how this critical position is spelled out in the setting of discourse about the Messiah in the Talmud of the Land of Israel. Bar Kokhba, above all, exemplifies arrogance against God. He lost the war because of that arrogance. In particular, he ignored the authority of sages:

Y. Taanit 4.5

[X J]   Said R. Yohanan, 'Upon orders of Caesar Hadrian, they killed eight hundred thousand in Betar.'

[K]   Said R. Yohanan, 'There were eighty thousand pairs of trumpeteers surrounding Betar. Each one was in charge of a number of troops. Ben Kozeba was there and he had two hundred thousand troops who, as a sign of loyalty, had cut off their little fingers.

[L]   Sages sent word to him, "How long are you going to turn Israel into a maimed people."

[M]   He said to them, "How otherwise is it possible to test them?"

[N]   They replied to him, "Whoever cannot uproot a cedar of Lebanon while riding on his horse will not be inscribed on your military rolls."

[O]   So there were two hundred thousand who qualified in one way, and another two hundred thousand who qualified in another way.

[P]   When he would go forth to battle, he would say, "Lord of the world! Do not help and do not hinder us! 'Hast thou not rejected us, O God? Thou dost not go forth, O God, with our armies'" [Ps. 60.10].

[Q]   Three and a half years did Hadrian besiege Betar.'

[R]   R. Eleazar of Modiin would sit on sackcloth and ashes and pray every day, saying 'Lord of the ages! Do not judge in accord with strict judgment this day! Do not judge in accord with strict judgment this day!'

[S]   Hadrian wanted to go to him. A Samaritan said to him, 'Do not go to him until I see what he is doing, and so hand over the city [of Betar] to you. [Make peace . . . for you.]'

[T]   He got into the city through a drain pipe. He went and found R. Eleazar of Modiin standing and praying. He pretended to whisper something in his ear.

[U]   The townspeople say [the Samaritan] do this and brought him to Ben Kozeba. They told him, 'We saw this man having dealings with your friend.'

[V]   [Bar Kokhba] said to him, 'What did you say to him, and what did he say to you?'

[W]   He said to [the Samaritan], 'If I tell you, then the king will kill me, and if I do not tell you, then you will kill me. It is better that the king kill me, and not you.

[X]   [Eleazar] said to me, "I should hand over my city." ["I shall make peace . . ."]'

[Y] He turned to R. Eleazar of Modiin. He said to him, 'What did this Samaritan say to you?'

[Z] He replied, 'Nothing.'

[AA] He said to him, 'What did you say to him?'

[BB] He said to him, 'Nothing.'

[CC] [Ben Kozeba] gave [Eleazar] one good kick and killed him.

[DD] Forthwith an echo came forth and proclaimed the following verse:

[EE] 'Woe to my worthless shepherd, who deserts the flock! May the sword smite his arm and his right eye! Let his arm by wholly withered, his right eye utterly blinded! [Zech. 11.17].

[FF] You have murdered R. Eleazar of Modiin, the right arm of all Israel, and their right eye. Therefore may the right arm of that man wither, may his right eye be utterly blinded!'

[GG] Forthwith Betar was taken, and Ben Kozeba was killed.

We notice two complementary themes. First, Bar Kokhba treats heaven with arrogance, asking God merely to keep out of the way. Second, he treats an especially revered sage with a parallel arrogance. The sage had the power to preserve Israel. Bar Kokhba destroyed Israel's one protection. The result was inevitable. The Messiah, the centerpiece of salvation history and hero of the tale, emerged as a critical figure. The historical theory of this Yerushalmi passage is stated very simply. In their view Israel had to choose between wars, either the war fought by Bar Kokhba or the 'war for Torah'. 'Why had they been punished? It was because of the weight of the war, for they had not wanted to engage in the struggles over the meaning of the Torah' (Y. Ta. 3.9 XVI I). Those struggles, which were ritual arguments about ritual matters, promised the only victory worth winning. Then Israel's history would be written in terms of wars over the meaning of the Torah and the decision of the law.

True, the skins are new, but the wine is very old. For while we speak of sages and learning, the message is the familiar one. It is Israel's history that works out and expresses Israel's relationship with God. The critical dimension of Israel's life, therefore, is salvation, the definitive trait, a movement in time from now to then. It follows that the paramount and organizing category is history and its lessons. In the Yerushalmi we witness, among the Mishnah's heirs, a striking reversion to biblical convictions about the centrality of history in the definition of Israel's reality. The heavy weight of prophecy, apocalyptic, and biblical historiography, with their emphasis upon salvation and on history as the indicator of Israel's salvation, stood against the Mishnah's quite separate thesis of what truly mattered. What, from their viewpoint, demanded description and analysis and required interpretation? It was the category of sanctification, for eternity. The true issue framed by history and apocalypse was how to move towards the foreordained end of salvation, how to act in time to reach salvation at the end of time. The Mishnah's teleology beyond time and its capacity to posit an eschatology without a place for a historical Mishnah take a position beyond that of the entire antecedent sacred literature of Israel. Only one strand, the priestly one, had ever taken so extreme a position on the centrality of sanctification and the peripheral nature of salvation. Wisdom had stood in between, with its own concerns, drawing attention both to what happened and to what endured. But to Wisdom what finally mattered was not nature or supernature, but rather abiding relationships in historical time.

The Talmud of Babylonia, at the end, carried forward the innovations we have seen in the Talmud of the Land of Israel. In the view expressed here, the principal result of Israel's loyal adherence to the Torah and its religious duties will be Israel's humble acceptance of God's rule. The humility, under all conditions, makes God love Israel.

> B. Hullin 89a
> 'It was not because you were greater than any people that the Lord set his love upon you and chose you' [Deut. 7.7]. The Holy One, blessed be he, said to Israel, 'I love you because even when I bestow greatness upon you, you humble yourselves before me. I bestowed greatness upon Abraham, yet he said to me, "I am but dust and ashes" [Gen. 18.27]; upon Moses and Aaron, yet they said, "But I am a worm and no man" [Ps. 22.7]. But with the heathen it is not so. I bestowed greatness upon Nimrod, and he said, "Come, let us build us a city" [Gen. 11.4]; upon Pharaoh, and he said, "Who are they among all the gods of the counties?" [II Kings 18.35]; upon Nebuchadnezzar, and he said, "I will ascend above the heights of the clouds" [Isa. 14.14]; upon Hiram, king of Tyre, and he said, "I sit in the seat of God, in the heart of the seas" [Ezek. 28.2].

So the system emerges complete, each of its parts stating precisely the same message as is revealed in the whole. The issue of the Messiah and the meaning of Israel's history framed through the Messiah myth convey in their terms precisely the same position that we find everywhere else in all other symbolic components of the rabbinic system and canon. The heart of the matter then is Israel's subservience to God's will, as expressed in the Torah and embodied in the teachings and lives of the great sages. When Israel fully accepts God's rule, then the Messiah will come. Until Israel subjects itself to God's rule, the Jews will be subjugated to pagan domination. Since the condition of Israel governs, Israel itself holds the key to its own redemption. But this it can achieve only by throwing away the key!

The paradox must be crystal clear: Israel acts to redeem itself through the opposite of self-determination, namely, by subjugating itself to God. Israel's power lies in its negation of power. Its destiny lies in giving up all pretence at deciding its own destiny. So weakness is the ultimate strength, forbearance the final act of self-assertion, passive resignation the sure step toward liberation (the parallel is the crucified Christ). Israel's freedom is engraved on the tablets of the commandments of God: to be free is freely to obey. That is not the meaning associated with these words in the minds of others who, like the sages of the rabbinical canon, declared their view of what Israel must do to secure the coming of the Messiah.

The passage, praising Israel for its humility, completes the circle begun with the description of Bar Kokhba as arrogant and boastful. Gentile kings are boastful; Israelite kings are humble. So, in all, the Messiah myth deals with a very concrete and limited consideration of the national life and character. The theory of Israel's history and destiny as it was expressed within that myth interprets matters in terms of a single criterion. What others within the Israelite world had done or in the future would do with the conviction that, at the end of time, God would send a (or the) Messiah to 'save' Israel, was a single idea for the sages of the Mishnah and the Talmuds and collections of scriptural exegesis. And that conception stands at the centre of their system; it shapes and is shaped by their system. In context, the Messiah expresses the system's meaning and so makes it work.

When constructing a systematic account of Judaism – that is, the world-view and way of life for Israel presented in the Mishnah – the philosophers of the Mishnah did not make use of the Messiah myth in the construction of a teleology for their system. They found it possible to present a statement of goals for their projected life of Israel which was entirely separate from appeals to history and eschatology. Since they certainly knew, and even alluded to, long-standing and widely held convictions on eschatological subjects, beginning with those in scripture, the framers thereby testified that, knowing the larger repertoire, they made choices different from others before and after them. Their document accurately and ubiquitously expresses these choices, both affirmative and negative.

Second, the appearance of a messianic eschatology fully consonant with the larger characteristic of the rabbinic system – with its stress on the viewpoints and proof-texts of Scripture, its interest in what was happening to Israel, its focus upon the national-historical dimension of the life of the group – indicates that the encompassing rabbinic system stands essentially autonomous of the prior, Mishnaic system. True, what had gone before was absorbed and fully assimilated, but the rabbinic system first appearing in the Talmud of the Land of Israel is different in the aggregate from the Mishnaic system. It represents more, however, than a negative response to its predecessor. The rabbinic system of the two Talmuds took over the fundamental convictions of the Mishnaic world-view about the importance of Israel's constructing for itself a life beyond time. The rabbinic system then transformed the Messiah myth in its totality into an essentially ahistorical force. If people wanted to reach the end of time, they had to rise above time, that is, history, and stand off at the side of great movements of political and military character. That is the message of the Messiah myth as it reaches full exposure in the rabbinic system of the two Talmuds. At its foundation it is precisely the message of teleology without eschatology expressed by the Mishnah and its associated documents. Accordingly, we cannot claim that the rabbinic or Talmudic system in this regard constitutes a reaction against the Mishnaic one. We must conclude, quite to the contrary, that in the Talmuds and their associated documents we see the restatement in classical-mythic form of the ontological convictions that had informed the minds of the second-century philosopher who produced the Mishnah. The new medium contained the old and enduring message: Israel must turn away from time and change, submit to whatever happens, so as to win for itself the only government worth having, that is, God's rule, accomplished through God's anointed agent, the Messiah. It is with the Talmud of the Land of Israel that Judaism becomes a messianic religion – but a messianic religion profoundly different from the other important religion of that classification, Christianity. For in the end, Judaism's Messiah was to be a sage, promising not the eschatological forgiveness of sins but the ultimate and entire sanctification of Israel: eternity now, eternity then, with little change from the one time to the other.

Notes

1. Documentation for the statements in this article will be found in these books of mine:
The Foundations of Judaism. Method, Teleology, Doctrine, Philadelphia 1983–5; *Messiah in Context. Israel's History and Destiny in Formative Judaism*, reissued in Studies in Judaism, Lanham, 1988; *Judaisms and their Messiahs in the beginning of Christianity* (with William Scott Green), New York 1987; *Ancient Judaism and Modern Category-Formation. 'Judaism', 'Midrash', 'Messianism', and Canon in the Past Quarter-Century*, Studies in Judaism, Lanham, 1986.

Messianism between Reason and Delusion: Maimonides and the Messiah

Marcel Poorthuis

'From Moses to Moses there was no one like Moses.' With these words Judaism honours the genius of Moses Maimonides, also called Rambam. Born on Pesach evening 1135 in Cordoba, he grew up to become a doctor, rabbi and philosopher. The mark of honour gives little indication how much already during his lifetime his work was at the centre of a controversy which could still spark off heated debates centuries after his death in 1204.

Maimonides' messianism can certainly also prompt differences of opinion within the Jewish tradition. He alternates quotations from reliable sources with daring interpretations in which above all honesty seems to be the guideline and the traditional substance of faith is subjected to thorough criticism.

1. The messianic expectation as a principle of faith

Maimonides gives the expectation of the messianic age an immovable position within his thirteen principles of faith. The twelfth principle relates to the days of the Messiah and affirms

> belief and firm trust in his coming and not to think that his coming is postponed. 'Although he tarry, wait for him' (Habakkuk 2.3). One may not fix any date for his coming nor hunt through Bible texts to establish the time of his coming.
>
> The wise men said, 'Cursed are they who calculate the end. We must

believe in him, honour and love him above all the kings of the world in accordance with what is prophesied about him from Moses to Malachi. And whoever doubts him or belittles his authority denies the Torah, which bears witness to him in Numbers 23–24 and Deuteronomy 30. This article of faith implies that a king over Israel will necessarily come from the house of David and from the descendants of Solomon. Whoever attacks the authority of this family denies God and the words of his prophet.[1]

Principles of faith do not have the same status within Judaism that the Christian creed has within Christianity. Jewish identity is not defined on the basis of a conviction of faith but on the basis of *halakhah* (the rules of the law). Moreover, the Talmud, the most authoritative (and very extensive) Jewish document, knows no creed or dogmas, and Maimonides' attempt at a 'creed' did not go uncriticized within Judaism. What prompted him to compose it, whether rival Muslim formulations and Christian claims to truth[2] or the need to put things in order in his own Jewish circle, may now be left out of account; the fact is that the content of the principles of faith reflects traditional views within Judaism. But the principles also have a colouring of their own.

In his categorical repudiation of all kinds of calculations of the time of the coming of the Messiah, Maimonides appeals to the Talmud. And indeed there are a number of powerful condemnations of 'apocalyptic' calculations in the Talmud tractate. However, this does show that such calculation was well established. Furthermore, even within the Talmud a whole series of speculations can be found, especially around the millennium, which for God is thought to be equivalent to one day of the week. Modern men and women may perhaps find numerical calculations of this kind somewhat remote, but they express the conviction that God will make the messianic peace dawn in his own way, even if reality does not seem to offer any kind of hope for it (indeed precisely then!). What we have here is a hope which does not have its basis in reality as that presents itself; there is no 'idolatry of the existing order', but a radical break with the evil and disaster that dominate the world and human beings. This conviction can help to keep believers going in misery and oppression, also out of a sense that the birth of the messianic age will be preceded by painful birth-pangs, disasters and wars, which are necessary but will only be temporary. However, there is also a reverse side to this 'impoverishment', namely that because hope is derived from God's intervention and not from human effort, it can lead to a denial of human freedom and to defeatism, when the time awaited has passed without the hoped-for success. This argument is also mentioned in the Talmud, against speculating with numbers: 'When the time has dawned without the Messiah having come, people will say that he will never come' (Babylonian Talmud, Sanhedrin 97b).[3]

Maimonides' messianism is rationalistic *par excellence*, and he has clearly made a selection from the richer Talmudic thought-material. He avoids interpreting the 'signs of the time', and refuses to see the birth-pangs which herald of the messianic age in catastrophes, as Sa'adya Gaon (882–942) did before him. He breaks a lance for human freedom and moral integrity, and rejects a deterministic scheme of history which can undermine the responsibility of the individual, although such determinism is given biblical and messianic legitimation.[4]

It is surprising to see how far Maimonides departs from the messianic expectations current among the people, which he sums up in his Commentary on Mishnah Sanhedrin X under five headings: some people believe literally in a land of milk and honey and in hell as a place of torture for the wicked; others think that the messianic life is an angelic existence; yet others that families will be reunited; a fourth group fulfils the commandments of the Torah in the expectation of being rewarded with prosperity here on earth; a fifth group combines all these elements.

Although all these views are based on the Torah, Maimonides seems to think them spiritually inferior. These people, the majority, take the stories in the Torah and the Talmud literally, and do not realize that the wise alluded to deep hidden wisdom in the form of parables. Those who reject the Torah also belong to the majority who do not understand the hidden wisdom and keep to the superficial, literal meaning. Here Maimonides seems to have in view 'positivistic' scholars *avant la lettre* who reject the Bible as being incompatible with science (cf. *Guide for the Perplexed* III, 43).[5]

However, Maimonides concludes that there is a very small group, or rather an individual here or there, capable of comprehending the wise men in the Talmud. It seems that in his thinking Maimonides counts himself among the 'happy few', but without wanting to disturb the masses.

In a parable Maimonides outlines the way to true, reasonable faith. When a child learns, he needs to be rewarded with sweets. When he gets bigger he will want clothes, and later still money, honour and respect. All this is necessary for motivation, but it is not the ultimate, pure motivation. Serving God is not ultimately aimed at one's own well-being, nor does it stem from the need for reward. To serve God and to fulfil the commandments for love of God is the purest form of faith. So Maimonides emphasizes the pedagogical character of the Bible, though this does not mean that the simple believer has to make do with untruths. 'Torah' itself means 'instruction' and thus leaves scope for different levels of insight; it offers not only the highest insight but also the way to it.

Still, we may note that for Maimonides the messianic expectation in its current form belongs more among the pedagogic truths than among the intrinsic truths (like the existence of God). Thus, paradoxical though it may seem, a hierarchy of truths is to be distinguished even *within* his principles of faith. Some centuries later the fifteenth-century Spanish Jewish philosopher Albo cut through the knot and stated that the coming of the Messiah was not among the foundations of Jewish faith, 'although it is appropriate to believe in it. However, for Christians it is a principle of faith, because their faith cannot be conceived without it' (*Ikkarim* I, 26; IV, 42).[6] It is probable that compulsory religious dialogue with Christians brought Albo to this minimalist standpoint; at any rate, in these 'conversations' he hammered home to Christians that without the Messiah their faith would have no meaning. However, to the present day there are prominent Jewish thinkers who develop their philosophy without a messianic expectation and for whom theocracy is the ideal, compared with which the rule of the Messiah remains only a fragile human endeavour.

For Maimonides, much that is all too human has crept in, especially into the ideas of the Messiah current among the people. His spiritual aristocracy comes clearly to the fore: there is a truth for the people and a truth for the individual thinker. On the basis of this, one can rightly ask how far for Maimonides the notion of the messianic time and of God who rewards and punishes (also one of his principles of faith) is not an outdated, primitive conception. However, if this should be the case, it would only be hinted at, as it were 'between the lines'.

In a famous study Leo Strauss suggests that literature which is written under the pressure of political or religious compulsion should be read by means of a special hermeneutic. In this literature, he argues, the generally accepted standpoint is amply presented, but the author's own opinion is not given. 'Between the lines', those in the know can trace the revolutionary new insights which escape the ordinary reader. The literary work which is written under 'persecution' therefore has an exoteric truth (accessible to all) and an esoteric truth (aimed at a small group of initiates).[7]

However, this hermeneutic is not applicable in all respects; at any rate, the thesis that the author's own opinion is to be found exclusively 'between the lines' largely escapes scientific verification and opens the door to the wildest speculation. Still, such an approach does illuminate certain contradictions in Maimonides' work, and applies not least to messianism. Maimonides relativizes current messianic notions and includes belief in the Messiah among the principles of faith: that is a first paradox that we have discovered.

2. The character of the messianic age

According to Maimonides, the prophetic promises of a wonderful age in which 'the wolf will lie down with the lamb' (Isaiah 11.6) do not point to a time of miracles, but are meant allegorically: the messianic age will be a time of peace and self-government for Israel. No people will rule over Israel any more, and all peoples will live in peace with Israel: 'the wolf with the lamb'.[8]

The wise men and prophets did not desire Israel's domination of the peoples nor even a life of eating and drinking to the full in the messianic age. It was their deepest wish that Israel should have freedom to study the Torah and to devote itself to wisdom without being plagued by oppression, and so become worthy of the 'world to come' (*Hilchot Melachim* [= Laws for Kings] 12.4).[9]

Physical, sensual pleasures do not fall within Maimonides' messianic perspective: he expects the highest rationality to coincide with an understanding of the mysteries of the Torah. The more that men are guided by rationality in their behaviour and no longer allow themselves to be led by instincts and to do violence to one another, the closer they are to the messianic reality. Maimonides rejects a miraculous transformation of catastrophe into salvation. Neither the natural laws nor the laws of the Torah will be changed in the messianic age.[10] Here Maimonides was challenging what was already a very old notion within Judaism, namely that the biblical commands and laws only have a temporary character and will be abolished in the messianic age. Early Christianity, and also the messianic movement of Shabbetai Zevi and Jakob Frank, were marked by this antinomian tendency. The expectation of a radical transformation of existence, of a radical break with the past which has more the character of a revolution than of a reform, fits in with this kind of religious feeling.

It seems that messianic expectation is reduced to a minimum in Maimonides. But there is one facet which comes strongly to the fore precisely because the miraculous features are largely lacking: messianism *as a political reality*, as an impact on society. For Maimonides, the person of the Messiah is an earthly ruler with political power who will gather the exiles to the land of Israel and wage war. However, he will not raise the dead and he is himself mortal like any other man. The messianic age means peace for Israel, a peace that can be guaranteed by political means. Self-government under a messianic king, a 'son of David', is not an other-worldly dream but a project of political autonomy to be realized. Zionism as the modern form of messianism and the return of the Jewish people to the political arena of states and peoples is connected with this venerable tradition of messianism as an amalgam of religious and political expecta-tion. It is an old and stubborn prejudice of Christian origin that Jewish messianism is too political to be able to reach the spiritual heights of the Christian messianic message. But we do better to follow Maimonides in asking whether a religious expectation which denies political oppression may bear the predicate 'messianic'.

The 'interpretation of catastrophes' does not fit in with this realistic political and philosophical view. Maimonides can detect no messianic trace and no progression towards the truth in the sheer ruination of reasonable-ness represented by calamities and wars. But here many Jews thought otherwise. We are well informed about them, thanks to a unique document, Maimonides 'Letter to the Jews in Yemen'. Here we can see clearly how the messianic expectation was a living reality, indeed even a matter of life and death, for the Jewish community and for Maimonides, who as well as being a philosopher was also a rabbi, and thus a spiritual leader.

3. The letter to the Jews in Yemen[11]

The letter to Yemen (1172) as Maimonides' answer to questions from the head of the Jewish community there. Since 1150 there had been a campaign by the Muslims to convert all non-Muslims forcibly to Islam. The situation in Yemen was further complicated by the fact that a Jewish apostate and missionary for Islam zealously argued that the Torah itself predicts the name of Muhammad. And to make things even worse, a messianic pretender had emerged who promised to free the Jews from oppression. These were the existential problems on which Maimonides' advice was asked.

Maimonides sees very clearly that this messianic movement has arisen because of the persecutions, and cannot be considered apart from them: religion as a reflection of social conditions. He himself explicitly writes in the letter: 'A drowning person clutches at a straw.' However, he does not stop at a rationalistic criticism of religion: a drowning man still remains a drowning man. Just to reject the 'straw' is no solution.

Maimonides boosts the morale of his readers by associating the actual suffering of the Jewish community with its call. It is because of their election that Jews have always been persecuted, and that is also the case now. The fight against the Jews is directed against God's election itself! So perseverance is not senseless, but an offering to God. Brute tyranny, but also subtle philosophical arguments, are the weapons by means of which people seek to part the Jews from their Torah. But this will be in vain. At present, Maimonides goes on to say, even religions like Islam and Christianity are attempting to combine both means through forced religious polemic. Jesus of Nazareth, 'may his bones turn to dust', interpreted the Torah in such a way as to abrogate its commands completely. Later the Romans appealed to him for a new religion (Christianity), though this was not his intent. After that came the Fool (= Muhammad).

According to Maimonides these two religions are indeed like the divine religion, but in the same way as a statue is like a living person.

After this diatribe, which gives vent to righteous indignation, the letter continues with a defence against the attempts of the above-mentioned apostate Jew to propagate Islam as the true religion. Texts like the promise of Moses of a 'prophet like me from among you, from your brethren' (Deut. 18.18) are wrongly cited as a proof for Muhammad. But the Muslims themselves proclaim that the Torah has been falsified. So why do they refer to it for proofs? Maimonides goes on to argue that biblical texts should not be taken out of context. Then it is clear that Moses' promise of a prophet 'like himself' refers to an Israelite, and that this certainly does not mean a prophet who will change the Torah.

Where Maimonides comes to speak of the Torah, he finds himself in an awkward situation. On the one hand he comforts the Jews of Yemen by pointing out that their suffering has meaning for the final redemption. Here he refers to the 'birth-pangs of the Messiah'; he encourages the Jews of Yemen by pointing out that these are temporary and will usher in redemption. On the other hand, however, he wants to disarm the messianic claims and refute numerical calculations about the impending redemption, yet without destroying the hope which keeps the Jews going. To take away the last straw would be a crime against the religious integrity of the Jews in Yemen and certainly cause a mass apostasy to Islam. However one looks at it, the messianic pretender has probably been successful in restoring their self-confidence to the Jews and giving religious meaning to the victims of persecution.

How does Maimonides go about things? He warns against over-hasty messianic movements and revolutionary actions, which often prove disastrous. Even at the Exodus, the classical model for the redemption, some Israelites who had calculated the time wrongly left too early and were killed (see Babylonian Talmud, Sanhedrin 92b).

Clearly the Jews in Yemen had mentioned numerical calculations to Maimonides; in this connection they even referred to the authority of Sa'adya Ga'on. But Maimonides refutes them in a bold way: Sa'adya Ga'on had to keep errant Jews on the way of truth and used numerical calculations as a pedagogical means, although he was well aware that they were illegitimate! He also rejects astrological calculations and refers to a prophecy of this kind which had recently been made in Andalusia: this did not bring the Messiah, but persecutions.

However, Maimonides does not stop at refutations, and here we come to one of the perplexing texts in his work. *He refers to a secret tradition in his family which contained the time of the restoration of prophecy (and perhaps of the coming of the Messiah)!* The numerical calculations, again based on the Exodus, point to the year 1216. Some scholars regard this text as a forgery, since it cannot be reconciled with everything that Maimonides teaches elsewhere. A forger is said to have been able to give his own scheme of chronology irrefutable authority by interpolating it into a letter of Maimonides. But this text is also already in the ancient versions of the letter, and an interpolation after 1216 would have made no sense. Moreover, it is probable that here Maimonides is using an extremely powerful argument to refute the messianic claims in Yemen and thereby to keep hope alive.[12]

Maimonides has few good words for the messianic pretender in Yemen. This man is undoubtedly deranged. He is more perplexed about the leader of the community, to whom he writes: 'How can you, as one who knows rabbinic teaching, follow him? . . . The Messiah stands above all men except Moses.'

The messianic pretender had called on people to give away all their possessions; Maimonides points out that the Talmud does not allow more than a fifth to be given away.

According to the tradition the Messiah will do miracles; Maimonides sees no mighty act by this pretender. This last argument is perhaps 'for the sake of the cause', since it is in tension with the minimal significance which Maimonides elsewhere attached to miracles in connection with the Messiah (see above). Moreover the Jews denied that the Messiah had supernatural properties and performed miracles as a defence against christological claims. So here the emphasis on the significance of miracle is clearly determined by the context. Moreover, in this connection the letter again refers to the political implications of messianism: kings and rulers will do miracles with authority.

Maimonides uses one last argument against this messianic pretender: immediately before the Messiah, false messiahs will emerge in large numbers. Maimonides (or a later copyist) gives several examples: one forecast a rain of blood, another leapt from tree to tree, but was condemned to death. 'But some believe that he is still kept hidden to this day . . .'

The end of the messianic pretender from Yemen, which Maimonides described years later, was also bizarre: 'He was taken captive by an Arab kind and said that he had done everything in truth and at God's behest. When the king asked for proof he said, "If you cut off my head, I shall be raised immediately." "There is no better proof!", exlaimed the king, and cut the poor beggar's head off. May his death bring reconciliation for himself and for all Israel . . . There are still fools who believe in his resurrection.'[13]

It is impressive in retrospect to read how Maimonides combines pastoral concern and philosophical insight. It would be quite wrong to see this letter only as a strategic document which does not contain Maimonides' own opinion as a thinker. Here he is wrestling with the question of the meaning of the suffering in all the persecutions and wants to associate the messianic hope with this. And who would want to deny that suffering for one's own religious identity can bring redemption nearer?

4. Maimonides on Christianity and Islam

The letter to Yemen, written to a community in distress and suffering under persecution, is not the place for a balanced description of the three monotheistic religions. But this document is also important for this subject; at any rate, the persecutions are an indisputable fact in the relationship between Judaism, Christianity and Islam. Elsewhere Maimonides gives a somewhat more balanced picture of this triangular relationship (*Mishneh Torah, Hilchot Melachim* 11, end). This text has been expunged from most manuscripts as a result of Christian censorship, but has been preserved in the Rome edition of 1480.

Jesus thought that he was the Messiah but was condemned to death . . . .
All the prophets promised that the Messiah would liberate Israel, bring

home the exiles and fulfil the commandments. He (Jesus) brought devastation upon Israel and humiliation upon 'the remnant'. He changed the Torah and led the world into the folly of serving another alongside God. However, it is not for the human spirit to fathom the plans of the Creator . . .

Everything connected with Jesus and the Ishmaelite Muhammad served only to prepare the way for the king Messiah, to bring the whole world to serve God with one mind. So the messianic expectation, the Torah and the commandments have become familiar topics of conversation as far as the distant islands among people without circumcision of heart and flesh.

Thus although Christianity and Islam are follies, their message of the one true God puts them in a messianic perspective. It is not given to any believer to grant the other religions a place on the way of the Messiah.

Maimonides turns the place of Christianity upside-down in an interesting way: it is not Judaism that is a preparation for Christianity, but Christianity is a first, imperfect way of acquainting the peoples with monotheism. Here we can already find echoes of the philosophy of Rosenzweig: Christianity must go through the world with its message on the way to the Father's house; Judaism is already with God the Father.

However, it is not sufficiently noted that Maimonides' vision serves a twofold purpose for Judaism itself: first, by referring to the spread of Christianity and Islam he can refute the notion that miracles are necessary to bring in the messianic time. Secondly, the stunning success of Christianity and Islam cannot be regarded as proof of the truth of these religions, as their adherents so fondly assert, but shows the glory of the message of Judaism. Although this message comes over in the other religions in a distorted form, its pedagogical value is important for a world which is sunk in idolatry.

So we need not attribute a complete recognition of the other religions to Maimonides, though some theologians in the Jewish-Christian dialogue want to do just that. What we do see is that Maimonides does not count the two religions, Christianity and Islam, as paganism, and this, given the Jewish experiences of persecution, is an indication of his spiritual aristocracy. However, the fundamental tolerance of messianism by Maimonides is not exclusive to him, but traditionally in Judaism rests on a fact that can still give Christianity food for thought: *for Maimonides* (and for the whole of rabbinic Judaism) *the world need not be Jewish in the messianic age*. A person must convert from idolatry and observe certain basic moral rules. If everyone behaves in a human way, the messianic reality is a fact. Such innocent openness to the human outside one's own confession, an openness which is not an acquisition of modern times but is rooted in the tradition itself, seems perhaps more difficult for Christianity to achieve.

Translated by John Bowden

Notes

1. Commentary on Mishnah Sanhedrin X. This text is to be found in traditional editions of the Talmud after tractate Sanhedrin. There is an English translation in F. Rosner, *Maimonides' Commentary on the Mishna: Sanhedrin*, New York 1981, and in J. Abelson, 'Maimonides on the Jewish Creed', *Jewish Quarterly Review* 19, 1907, 24–58, reprinted in J. I. Dienstag, *Eschatology in Maimonidean Thought*, New York 1983.

2. This 'external' view is followed by many scholars, but disputed by A. Hyman, 'Maimonides' Thirteen Principles', in A. Altmann (ed.), *Jewish Medieval and Renaissance Studies*, Cambridge, Mass. 1967, 136–44.

3. A good translation of the Talmud is I. Epstein (ed.), *The Babylonian Talmud*, Soncino Edition, London 1950ff.

4. For what is undoubtedly the most thoroughgoing philosophical interpretation of messianism as a dialectic of freedom and constraint see E. Levinas, *Difficile Liberté*, Paris [2]1976, 95–106. My dissertation *Het gelaat van de Messias*, to be defended at the end of 1992, has a translation of and commentary on these texts.

5. See the translation by S. Pines, *The Guide for the Perplexed*, Chicago 1963.

6. See the text and translation in I. Husik (ed.), *Sefer Ha'Ikkarim/Book of Principles*, Philadelphia 1929.

7. See the essay 'Persecution and the Art of Writing', in Leo Strauss, *Persecution and the Art of Writing*, Westport 1976, 25, 29, 30, 36. See also 'The Literary Character of the Guide for the Perplexed', ibid., especially 83. D. Hartman, *Maimonides: Torah and Philosophic Quest*, Philadelphia 1976, 20–7, has a more harmonizing approach.

8. Such allegorizing would later be attacked from two sides, on the one hand for damaging the supernatural nature of the prophetic promises (thus Nachmanides) and on the other for transforming the biblical narratives into a philosophical tractate in disguise, in order to 'rescue' the Bible before the tribunal of philosophy (Spinoza).

9. See the translation by A. M. Hershman, *The Code of Maimonides, XIV (The Book of Judges)*, New Haven [2]1963.

10. Here Maimonides is less laconic than it seems. The Messiah will rebuild the temple and restore sacrifice. But in the philosophical work *The Guide for the Perplexed* sacrifice is no more than a pedagogical means for putting the people, plunged deeply into idolatry, on the way of monotheism,. Here too a tension is evident.

11. The best edition of the Arabic original and three Hebrew translations is A. S. Halkin, *Iggeret Teman: Moses Maimonides' Epistle to Yemen*, New York

1952. See also his annotated translation with an extensive commentary by D. Hartman in *Crisis and Leadership: Epistles of Maimonides*, New York 1985, 91–207.

12. See Halkin, *Iggeret Teman* (n. 11), introduction, xii.

13. Leter to Marseilles. Cf. J. I. Dienstag, Introduction, 'Persons Associated with the Eschatological Teachings of Maimonides', in id., *Eschatology in Maimonidean Thought*, New York 1983, lxxiv, xl.

The Messianism of Shabbetai Zevi and Jewish Mysticism

Marcus van Loopik

'I am the Lord your God, Shabbetai Zevi.' Such was the name adopted by the pseudo-Messiah Shabbetai Zevi (1626–1676), who for a short time was the centre of one of the greatest messianic movements in Jewish history. Many accounts of his person are historical and descriptive. Here, however, I want above all to explore the roots and background of his thought and explain why his contemporaries were so receptive to his messianic claims.

Kabbalah, Torah and tradition

Like the other great religions, Judaism, too, has mystical traditions. These are usually denoted by the term *kabbalah*, from the Hebrew verb *kabal* = receive.

In contrast to non-Jewish mysticism, Jewish mysticism is rarely about personal experience of God. Jewish mysticism is far more than personal testimony; it is the spiritual legacy of a historical community. Certainly, striving towards mystical and personal experience, and towards union with God, in later terminology called 'cleaving' (*debequt*) to God, is an indispensable part of Jewish mysticism, but it is no more than that. Most of Jewish mysticism is devoted to mystical exegesis of scripture, theosophy, cosmogony, esoteric knowledge and visionary descriptions of the heavenly world. In the Talmudic period (around 0–500 CE) the most usual terms to denote Jewish mysticism were *ma'aseh bereshit* (investigating the mysteries of the process of creation, with the beginning of the book of Genesis as a starting point), and *ma'aseh merkabah* (the description of God's throne and heavenly abodes, with the first visionary chapter of Ezekiel and the sixth chapter of Isaiah as a starting point). The relationship between Jewish mysticism and the revelation on Sinai emerges from the close link between Jewish mystical literary sources and exegesis of scripture. Old Talmudic terms for mystical traditions are *sod* (the hidden meaning of the Torah), *razei torah* (mysteries of the Torah), and *sitrei Torah* (secrets of the Torah). Mystics are called *ba'alei sod*, literally 'possessors of the mystery'.

The mystical practice of rising above the world of material conceptions to be closer to God has always been bound up with the Jewish tradition as a whole and to a not unimportant extent also with the *halakhah*, i.e. with the knowledge and practice of the commandments (*mitzwot*). To try to practise kabbalistic meditation without a thorough knowledge of the foundation of Jewish mysticism in the Torah is like trying to fly without wings.[1] The most characteristic feature of the Jewish mystical path is that one cannot make any advance in meditation without a corresponding discipline in the world of action, and without fulfilling the commandments revealed by God. The seven heavenly palaces which according to age-old tradition the mystic enters one after the other on his way to the heavenly throne were at a very early stage identified with the path of the virtues.[2]

The world below and the world above

A central notion in Jewish mysticism is the correspondence between heavenly and earthly reality. Everything that is on earth is a reflection of the heavenly world above.[3] This correspondence rests on a basic pattern that heaven and earth have in common and that is connected with the mystical and hidden meaning of the Torah. In rabbinic tradition the Torah is described as the instrument by which the world is created. When God created his world, he first looked in the Torah as an architect first consults his blueprint before beginning to build.[4] The crux of this comparison is that the whole universe rests on a religious, ethical and ritual order which is connected with the being of God and is fulfilled by God's will. The experience that everything is permeated by the world above became determinative for the sense of life among the Kabbalists. The notion of the Torah as the basic plan of the world becomes *the* point of contact for mystical speculation about God's relation to his creation. In the Mishnah (compiled by Rabbi Jehuda ha-Nasi around 210 CE, Abot V.1), we find a saying which laid the foundation for much of later mystical speculation:

By ten Sayings (*'asarah ma'amarot*) was the world created. And what does the Scripture teach thereby? Could it not have been created by one Saying? But this was to requite the ungodly which destroy the world that was created by ten sayings, and to give a goodly reward to the righteous which sustain the word that was created by ten Sayings (Danby, *Mishnah*, 455).

The world rests on a moral order, and anyone who destroys this draws down heavy guilt upon himself. Of course it was asked what the true nature of this order is and what the ten sayings from this tradition are. In an interpretation attributed to Rab (Rab Abba ben Aibu, from Babylonia, third century),[5] which is possibly akin to mystical ideas, the ten sayings were identified with divine properties (*middot*).[6] The *middot* (properties) of God were later also personified[7] and imagined as intermediary phases in the creation of visible reality. They form the archetypes of creation. These ideas are worked out further in mystical writings like *Sepher Yetzirah* (Book of the Creation),[8] *Sepher ha-Bahir* (Book of the Shining [Light]),[9] and *Sepher ha-Zohar* (Book of the Splendour).[10] The emanated divine properties are there called *sephirot*, a name which probably originally meant 'numbers', but later took on the significance of 'emanations'.[11] In contrast to Neo-Platonic conceptions, the *sephirot* do not form a real hierarchy. Their dynamic relations form the symbolic description of processes which make up part of God's being. In their mutual relations the *sephirot* are depicted in the form of an upside-down tree (with its roots in heaven), and in later traditions above all as a transcendent human being, the *'Adam Qadmon* (the Man Before the World, of whom all our material reality and especially man as a microcosm form a reflection).

A connection is made with the world of human action by the idea that the correspondence between above and below is not static, but that the two worlds constantly interact with each other. This interaction is governed by the Torah. Each letter of the Torah is connected with the structure of the earthly and heavenly reality, and the fulfilment of the commandments, prayer and study have direct consequences for the harmony in the world of the *sephirot* and thus indirectly for the earthly reflection of it. Mysticism and observance of the commandments here go hand in hand.

Mysticism and messianism

Jewish mysticism is not only a flight from the pains and limitations of changeable and perishable history into the perfect, incorruptible and unchangeable world of the spirit. Although the Jewish mystic seeks comfort in proximity to God and at the same time looks away from the bloody terrors of history, turning his eye inward, to 'in the beginning' and to what is above, he remains an inhabitant of the earth, physically bound up with the historical community. He studies the *halakhah*, in which the historical and social guidelines for the functioning of this society are given. He shares in the messianic longing, and together with his people prays for the redemption of the world and the return of his people to Eretz Yisrael. From of old, Jewish mysticism and messianic longing have been linked. The mystic directs his gaze not only upwards and to the beginning of creation, but also to the end of times and to the future of Israel.[12] In a number of mystical traditions about a meditative journey by the mystic to the seventh heaven and God's throne, there is the prospect of the future return of Israel from the Diaspora and the rebuilding of the Temple.[13] The world of the *sephirot*, of the emanated divine properties, is not a static world, but the reflection of the earthly and historical process of redemption.

In Luria's thought, the whole of visible and invisible reality is experienced as a messianic process. The world of the *sephirot*, which serves as a heavenly model for the earthly reality that has been created out of nothing, came into being after the Infinite One withdrew into himself from one point. This process of God's contraction is called *zimzum* (withdrawal, limitation). Through the idea of *zimzum* it is possible to experience creation as a process in God and at the same time as an independent reality over against God. The emanation of the *sephirot* of the upper world took place in the 'space' which came about within God through his self-contraction. In Luria's original thought this emanation is a process of purification in God, who thus purged himself of the 'roots of judgment', characteristics of evil. It is not revelation, but withdrawal and hiddenness, which form the real beginning of God's creative move outwards. This mystical vision takes up the strongly emotional experience of God's hiddenness and absence from history and offers comfort with the insight that the hiddenness of God is inherent in creation.

However, during the process of creation a catastrophe took place, the *shebirah*, 'the breaking of the vessels'. The world of the *sephirot* could not withstand the power of the divine emanation, and the 'vessels' which had to give 'form' to the emanated light broke, one after the other. The harmony of the world of the *sephirot* was destroyed and along with it the harmony of God's Holy Name, the Tetragrammaton. Until the lost unity of God's name is restored, Israel must remain in exile. The light that the 'vessels' could not contain streamed through the break, and there was a quite unbridgable gap between the Infinite One (God in his utmost unknowability) and spiritual and earthly reality. Human beings live in a broken world. As a consequence of the break, sacred sparks of the divine light descended into the world of material creation and were caught up in the *kelippot* (shells) produced by the fragmenting of the vessels and making the evil purged from God. As a consequence of a cosmic catastrophe the harmony of the archetypal upper world has been destroyed, and with it also the harmony of visible reality. Although the fall of Adam – which at the same time is a model for anyone who falls – increased the rupture in creation, this brokenness at the same time also transcends human responsibility. The brokenness is inherent in God's creation and at the same time imposes an obligation to bring about the process of purification. Here suffering and exile take on meaning and significance.

There is a process of *tikkun* (restoration) in the world above, and it is the responsibility of human beings to complete this process of redemption by the influence that human actions have on that world. Simultaneously with the restoration of the world above and of God's name, and the repair of the break between the shekinah (God's presence on earth) and its origin, God's will and creative potential will once again be able to stream unhindered through visible reality and an end will come to human suffering and to Israel's exile. In Luria's mysticism, Israel's exile is experienced as a command to Israel to descend to the lowest levels and liberate God's banished sparks from their impure lodging. Here Israel accomplishes a divine and cosmic process of purification.

The thought-world of Yizhaq Luria and Shabbetai Zevi

We have already established that a focus on messianic expectations of the future was always the essential characteristic of Jewish mysticism, although it was not its central point. In the sixteenth-century world of Yizhaq Luria, however, the messianic longing came to stand at the centre of mystical reflection. The ideas of Yizhaq Luria, the great mystic from the Safed group,[14] populated the thought world of the messianic mystic Shabbetai Zevi. A summary description of Lurias's Kabbala and some historical observations are necessary if we are to understand the life and thought-world of Shabbetai Zevi.

Particular events in the sixteenth century provided a new impulse towards messianic reflection. In the year 1492 – the very year in which redemption was expected[15] – the Jews were expelled from Spain, and in 1498 from Portugal. Large groups of refugees spread from these countries over Northern Europe and the Mediterranean and integrated themselves into other Jewish communities, bringing with them a great legacy of philosophical and above all mystical traditions. From this time the influence of the Kabbala becomes evident in all Jewish communities. In the world of the Kabbala, accents were shifted. The vision and description of an eternal and higher reality was more closely and more deliberately bound up with apocalyptic and messianic concerns.[16]

A forerunner of this mystical development was Moshe Cordovero (1552–1570), who came from Spain. He was one of the greatest mystics, and belonged to the intimate circle of mystics – the *haberim* (associates) – of Safed in northern Israel. Moshe Cordovero developed very systematic- ally a number of practical exercises in mystical meditation by which man, as a microcosm, could combine the divine properties within himself, in his thought, action and words, and bring himself inner rest and harmony. This harmony leads to humility and self-denial, and forms the preparation for a meditative approach to God. Since the properties in human beings correspond to the world of the *sephirot*, in his action and experience the mystic at the same time brings about harmony and integration in the transcendent word of the *sephirot* and throughout creation. In fact no distinction is made here between daily actions and meditations.[17]

The ideas of Moshe Cordovero bore abundant fruit in the thought of his great contemporary Yizhaq Luria (1534–72), who also came to Safed. In line with his practical meditations, Luria constructed a whole system of exercises in concentration (*kawwanot*) for prayer and daily life (*kawwanot*), and he gave mystical experience an all-embracing 'messianic' and dynamic significance. In Luria, practical concern for furthering the process of redemption through action, prayer and study is placed at the centre of theoretical reflection by means of the concept of *tikkun* (restoration).[18] In this way Luria gave Kabbalistic thought as a whole a messianic orientation. The characteristic difference between Luria's mysticism and older Kabbalistic mysticism is that whereas in the last the divine emanations are more or less static, in Luria's Kabbala emanation has a markedly dynamic character.[19]

In this view, however, the person of the Messiah is not really a decisive factor on the way to cosmic redemption; any human deed can help the Shekinah to liberate both the divine sparks sunk and fallen in the world below and itself. The Messiah will come only if with the help of Israel the good has overcome the evil in the world.[20] In the words of Gershom Scholem: 'For Luria, the coming of the Messiah means no more than the signature on a document that we ourselves write.'[21] The soul of the

Messiah will only be born in the unifying of the *sephirot* who were separated by the cosmic break. In later Kabbala influenced by Luria – in Shabbetai Zevi –, building on the notion of a being of the Messiah emerging from the upper world, we find by contrast a development of the idea that only the Messiah will be in a state to release the last and most deeply sunk sparks from their exile. Thus his contribution to the process of redemption is held to be indispensable.

Shabbetai Zevi, life and thought

The Thirty Years' War in the seventeenth century produced a large number of victims and an unprecedented depth of poverty. Where there was little to share, xenophobia increased. Bitter economic competition developed, against and among Christian guilds, from which the Jews had been excluded. The atmosphere of hatred and envy led to pogroms in Frankfurt (1614) and Worms (1615). In 1648–9 a rebellion of Cossacks under the leadership of Khmielnitzki and aided by the Tatars led to a scourge of murder and plundering of the Jews in Poland, where they became the victims of the hatred produced by feudal exploitation, though this was no fault of theirs. These centuries were the heyday of magic and delusion, and the climate was favourable for belief in the pseudo-messiah Shabbetai Zevi to put down roots. The seed of messianic hope fell in the dark but fruitful earth of a desperate diaspora to grow and bear fruit in an unprecedented way.

Although I mean here above all to discuss the religious background to Shabbetai's movement, in passing I would like to give some biographical details, since the life and thought of Shabbetai Zevi formed an indissoluble unity. Shabbetai Zevi was born in Izmir in 1626. At an early age he acquired great knowledge of the *halakhah*, and at eighteen he was given the official title of *hakam*.[22] However, at an early stage he also showed signs of a manic-depressive psychosis which to the end of his life was to toss him from periods of ecstatic exuberance to periods of depression in which he withdrew into silence. These alternating periods were described by his pupils as times of divine inspiration alternating with times of concealment, in which he entered into battle with the cosmic powers of evil in order to redeem the banished divine sparks. In 1648, the year forecast in the Zohar for the coming of the Messiah, Shabbetai for the first time gave clear hints that he was at least the unique herald of the redemption of Israel by uttering the Tetragrammaton publicly,[23] as a symbolic uniting of the letters of God's name which had been separated along at the cosmic exile.

Shabbetai claimed to have a unique relationship with 'the God of Israel', and through his visionary and prophetic gifts to have a share in *sod ha'elohut*, the divine mystery. The so-called *ma'assim zarim* (strange actions), were one striking feature in his life-style, manipulated by prophetic inspirations. These were actions contrary to the *halakhah* to which Shabbetai felt himself compelled by inspiration from on high. Because his behaviour gave offence, around 1651 he was expelled from Izmir by the Jewish authorities. In 1662, after much travelling, he reached Jerusalem, and after spending some years in Cairo, in April 1665 he met Abraham Natan ben Elishah Hayyim Ashkenazy, better known as Nathan of Gaza, for short. This encounter with the prophet from Gaza, who had the reputation of being able to disclose the hidden roots of any soul, was to be crucial for the rise of a messianic movement which was to bring large parts of Jewry to ecstasy and to bitter disillusionment. Like many others, Shabbetai travelled to Gaza in order to have the secrets of his soul disclosed by the prophet and to restore the broken relationship with his spiritual roots. Even before he came, Nathan received a vision in which he saw that the name Shabbetai was engraved as the Messiah in heavenly spheres. On the basis of this experience he tried to convince Shabbetai of his task as the messianic redeemer. This proved successful, for on 17 Siwan 1665 Shabbetai proclaimed himself the Messiah and the redeemer of Israel. This proclamation marked the official beginning of Shabbetai's movement. The rumor of it spread like wildfire, first in the East and then in the West. The time was ripe for it.

At the end of 1665, Nathan of Gaza wrote a letter to Raphaël Joseph, the leader of the Egyptian Jews. This letter can be regarded as *the* manifesto of Shabbetai's movement. In the first part of the letter the writer judged that mankind stood on the threshold of a new age, in which the wingbeats of the world to come could already be heard. In his view, the time of the Lurian *kawwanot* (the prayers and commandments laid down with special intention for the restoration of the world of the *sephirot*) had ended. The transcendental restoration of the world of the *sephirot* was almost complete and the breakthrough of redemption now depended only on the ultimate action of the Messiah. One new idea was that the Lurian process of *tikkun* can no longer bring the whole transcendent world above to redemption by means of obedience to the Torah, but only helps the uppermost world. The lowest half of the world of creation can only be liberated by the Messiah himself, whose (divine) soul from the beginning of God's *zimzum* (self-limitation) already descended to the lowest regions, there to pit himself against the powers of evil. The Messiah must defile himself in order to free the sacred sparks which have sunk lowest, and therefore is not subject to the regime of the Torah.

Nathan divided the world age into three parts: 1. the working week of six working days and the time of the *shebirah* (the cosmic break), and the necessary *tikkun* (restoration by deliberate human action); 2. *'ereb Shabbat*, the time which directly precedes the Sabbath and which forms a transitional period between that and the time of exile; and 3. the time of real redemption, the Sabbath. With the Sabbath, the day of rest and redemption has dawned. The time of the Sabbath forms the transitional period in which the Sabbath itself has not yet begun, but in which the work of the week no longer needs to be done fully. Anyone who still holds firm to the *kawwanot* must be regarded as one who keeps on working when the Sabbath dawns. The most important criterion for human judgment now no longer lies in his actions but in his messianic faith, which is none other than faith in the redemptive activities of Shabbetai Zevi. Only the believers (*ma'aminim*), as the followers of Shabbetai call themselves, will have a share in the world to come. All this represented a spiritualization and individualization of the national messianic future ideal alien to the nature of rabbinic Judaism (according to the traditional view, all Israel shares in the world to come).[24]

In the Kabbala the idea is that the nature of the Messiah derives from the world above and that he has the same soul as Adam, David and Moses. The consonants of the name Adam already point to the unity of the three persons. It is remarkable how this idea of the supernatural being of the Messiah, whose soul issued from the world of the *sephirot* to liberate the last banished sparks of the Shekinah, could degenerate into the deification of a man identified with the Messiah. From indications in his correspondence it is evident that Shabbetai Zevi identified himself with Adam Qadmon, incarnate in a human person; in mysticism Adam Qadmon is the symbol for the God who manifests himself in creation.[25] It is notable how the idea current in Jewish mysticism of the unveiling of a deeper mystical exposition of the Torah in the messianic period in Shabbetai Zevi degenerated into a more or less antinomian attitude.[26] This represented an unprecedented break with traditional Jewish mysticism. It was precisely in the 'alien actions' of transgression that Shabbetai saw a means towards *tikkun*. This antinomian aspect of Shabbetai's religious ideas in particular explains the long-lasting attraction of the movement.[27] In 1666 Shabbetai himself spoke the blessing, 'Blessed are you, Lord, who authorize the forbidden.'[28] In the first instance the forbidden deeds were explicitly allowed only to the Messiah himself (as in an antinominan tractate of

Abraham Miguel Cardoso).[29] In a small circle, transgressions of the law were already propagated during the lifetime of Shabbetai himself,[30] but larger groups quickly sprang up here and there in which antinomianism was practised. Thus in Turkey Jacob Querido, who was supposed to have the soul of the Messiah ben Joseph, preached lawlessness and immorality. The tendency towards lawlessness culminated in the openly antinomian movement around Jakob Frank (1726–1791). This movement above all influenced groups in the Balkans.

On 15 September 1666, Sultan Mehmed IV gave Shabbetai the choice of death or conversion to Islam. With Shabbetai's conversion to Islam the Sultan hoped to put an end to the political unrest which his appearance caused and moreover to be able to convert large groups of Jews to Islam along with him. Shabbetai chose life and officially went over to Islam. In reality, however, he remained the centre of the Jewish messianic movement and down to his death he caused excitement with numerous prophetic inspirations.

Until well into the eighteenth century, the ideas and claims of Shabbetai Zevi, the eventual convert to Islam, and references to his person were to retain their virulence. This was possible because Nathan of Gaza interpreted Shabbetai's move to Islam as a necessary descent to the lowest levels of reality in order also to liberate the 'sparks' which had fallen lowest.[31] Nathan interpreted Shabbetai's death, at a moment when redemption had not yet become historical reality, as a merely temporal hiddenness and withdrawal of the Messiah into the world of the *sephirot*. Thus his death became a complement to his divinization. Especially in Germany and Poland, the success of this rationalization of Shabbetai's apostasy was evident from the pseudo-Shabbetaian prophets and messiahs who appeared everywhere. The attraction and durability of Shabbetai's movement can only be explained from the great emphasis in Luria's Kabbala on human initiative. His followers tried to hasten on the process of *tikkun* by the study of mystical works, prayer and asceticism. *The real driving force was the experience of not being handed over involuntarily to circumstances but being able to make a breakthrough in the process of redemption on one's own initiative. Redemption was no longer a promise for the remote future, but a happening which could be brought within reach.*

Although I am not suggesting any historical relationship, the parallel with Christian theology is obvious. There too a historical person with messianic claims is divinized, and there too the binding obligations of the Torah and oral tradition are denied. The theology around Shabbetai also sought explanations for his behaviour, his death and the failure of historical redemption still to come. The answer that Christianity – which became a world religion – gave to the life and death of Jesus, especially as a result of the changed attitude to Torah and oral tradition, represented a rejection of the Jewish roots from which it had come. Shabbetai's movement could not survive within rabbinic Judaism, which in principle maintained the authority of scripture and tradition. The movement was doomed to go under as a pseudo-messianic movement; its ideas may have derived from those of Jewish mysticism, but were distorted in dispute with the nature of traditional Jewish mysticism. Shabbetai and his followers robbed of its force the traditional bond with the *halakhah* and divinized the Messiah. What the Shabbetai movement did share with the traditional messianic expectation of the future was the nationalistic element: the desire cherished for long ages to return to the land of Israel and the belief – despite expressions of antinomianism – that this could be brought about by repentance and prayer.

Translated by John Bowden

Notes

1. See P. Epstein, *Kabbalah – The Way of the Jewish Mystic*, Boston and London 1978, reprinted 1988, xvii.

2. See G. Scholem, 'Ma'aseh Merkabah 9', in *Jewish Gnosticism*, 107; Scholem dates the origin of this interpretation to the third century, see id., 'Kabbalah', *Encyclopaedia Judaica* X, 505. The relationship between mysticism and *halakhah* emerges above all from the demand that is made on the mystic in the old mystical writings, see e.g. a passage from Hekhalot Rabbati (the dating of the *hekhalot* texts, i.e. a number of mystical texts with a description of God's heavenly palaces [*hekhalot*] is disputed, but it is certain that their content goes back to the first centuries. For the problem of the dating see D. Halperin, *The Face of the Chariot*, Tübingen 1988, ch. IX; Hebrew text in A. J. Wertheimer, *Battei Midrashot* I, Jerusalem 1950, 67–136): 'He alone is a Yored Merkabah (someone who 'descends' and has a vision of the heavenly chariot), who has these characteristics: who reads and learns Torah, prophets and writings . . . who does and heeds all the Torah: all ordinances, laws, prescriptions and instructions which were said to Moses on Sinai.' For this and other passages see N. A. van Uchelen, *Joodse Mystiek, Merkawa, Tempel en Troon*, Amsterdam 1983, 69–84.

3. See Shemot Rabbah XXXIII.4 (ed. Wilna Romm, reprinted Jerusalem 1961): 'Rabbi Berekhiah opened (an interpretation with the Torah quotation): "Yours, Lord, is the greatness, the power, the glory, the splendour and the majesty, indeed all that is in heaven and earth" (I Chron. 29.11). Here you find the proof that the Holy One, Blessed be He, created everything above and below . . .'

4. See Bereshit Rabbah I.1 (ed. J. Theodor and C. Albeck, reprinted Jerusalem 1965); compare traditions according to which the world was created for the sake of the Torah: Siphre, 'Eqeb 37 (ed. L. Finkelstein, reprinted New York 1969); Bereshit Rabbah I.4; Wayyiqra Rabbah XXXIII.3 (ed. M. Margulies, Jerusalem 1985), etc.

5. bHagigah 12a (ed. Wilna-Romm).

6. 1. ḥokmah (wisdom), 2. tebunah (insight), 3. da'at (knowledge), 4. koah (strength), 5. ga'arah (reprimand, i.e. setting limits), 6. geburah (courage or moral power), 7. ṣedeq (righteousness), 8. mishpat (right judgment), 9. ḥesed (steadfast love). 10. raḥamim (mercy).

7. See 'Abot de Rabbi Natan XXXVII, nosach a (55b, ed. S. Schechter, reprinted New York 1967), referring to Hos. 2.21–22 [18–19]: 'Seven middoth do service before the Throne of Glory, and these are they: wisdom, righteousness and judgment, steadfast love and mercy, truth and peace.'

8. Written between the third and the sixth centuries. According to a tradition in bSanhedrin 65b, Rab Hanina and Rab 'Oshaya (two Babylonian scholars and brothers, end of the third/beginning of the fourth century) were occupied with the Sepher Yetzirah (in manuscripts and sources also Hilkhot Yetzirah); it is not improbable that the reference here is to the primal form of what we know as Sepher Yetzirah. For Sepher Yetzirah see the discussion in Gershom Sholem, Kabbalah, 23–30.

9. Presumably composed in the twelfth century, and partly based on the work Razza Rabba, which dates from the end of the Gaonite period. It came from Babylonia, but was lost, and only fragments are known from the sources of mediaeval Ashkenasy Hasidism. For a short description of Sepher ha-Bahir see Gershom Sholem, Kabbalah, 312–16.

10. The main part of this work is a mystical commentary on the Torah. It was composed at the end of the thirteenth century and was attributed to Rabbi Mosheh ben Shem Tob de Leon (died 1305). Later, various parts were added: for the extremely complex composition and history of the redaction see G. Scholem, 'Zohar', Encyclopaedia Judaica XVI, 1193–215.

11. See Scholem, Encyclopaedia Judaica X, 565. In Sepher ha-Bahir and Sepher ha-Zohar the sephirot are developed into a connected system of emanated divine properties. In these writings above all an ethical order is seen in the world of the sephirot, and a relationship is established with God's middot (properties). Other terms are: kochot (powers, potencies), shemot (names: the ephirot are also identified with different divine names), orot (lights), dibburim (words of divine revelation), ma'amarim (statements), lebushim (garments), madregot (steps), ketarim (crowns).

12. This relationship between mysticism and future expectation is already established in the Mishnah (Hagigah II.1), in a warning to mystics.

13. Here I would refer above all to the so-called hekhalot texts (see n. 2 above); on these see G. Scholem, Die jüdische Mystik in ihren Hauptströmungen, reprinted Frankfurt am Main 1980, 79 and 400 n. 115; N. A. van Uchelen, Joodse Mystiek – Merkaba – Tempel en Troon, 61ff. See also the relationship between God's emanated middot (properties) and the messianic future expectation in Pirqe de-Rabbi Eli'ezer (a Midrash text, the redaction of which took place between 640 and 900), end of ch. III.

14. A place in Galilee where a small community of Jewish mystics settled in the sixteenth century.

15. Scholem, Die jüdische Mystik, 269 and 439 n. 4.

16. See the comments by Scholem, *Die jüdische Mystik*, 269–75, see also id., *The Messianic Idea*, New York 1971, 41f.

17. For a brief classification and description of the background to the meditation techniques of Moshe Cordovero see P. Epstein, *Kabbalah*, 14–17.

18. See Scholem, *Die jüdische Mystik*, 284: all Kabbala has practical aspects, but the way in which practice and theory are related in Luria's concept of *tikkun* is unique.

19. See M. Pozen, 'Tephisat ha-Historia be-'Einei ha-Kabbalah', in *Chebrah we-Historia*, ed. E. Cohen, Jerusalem 1980, 526. See J. Liebes, 'Ha-Mashiach shel ha-Zohar li-Demuto ha-Meschichi shel Rabbi Shim'on bar Jochai', in *Ha Ra'jon ha-Meschichi be-Jisrael*, ed. S. Ram, Jerusalem 1982, 103, 107. He sees the difference between the thought of Cordovero and that of Luria in terms of the difference between a static and a dynamic view of the world.

20. See Scholem, *Kabbalah*, 67, referring to the *Etz Hayim* of Hayim Vital (1542–1620); see also Scholem, *Sabbatai Sevi*, Princeton 1973, 48.

21. 'For Luria the coming of the Messiah means no more than the signing of a document which we ourselves write' (Scholem, *Zur Kabbala*, 157). Cf. Id., *Die jüdische Mystik*, 301–2. In Luria's school, different standpoints can be recognized in relation to the question whether an active appearance of the Messiah is needed to free the last spark (see Scholem, *Kabbalah*, 168).

22. See H. J. Schoeps, *Jüdische Geisteswelt*, Darmstadt nd, 176, referring to a report in Rabbi Ya'aqob Emden (1697–1776); see further sources there, with bibliographical information (176–87).

23. Despite the strict prohibition against doing this: see bYom.69b, bSot.38a, etc. For Shabbetai's action see Scholem, *Kabbalah*, 247, and *Die jüdische Mystik*, 320 (and 448 n. 12). Under the influence of Nathan of Gaza, Shabbetai officially proclaimed himself Messiah in 1665. He stated that 15 Siwan 1666 would be the day of redemption; for this see Scholem, *Kabbalah*, 254; cf. also P. Schäfer, *Emuna*, V/VI, 1974, 342.

24. For the theology of Shabbetai Zevi see Y. Jacobson, *Mi Kabbalat ha-Ari 'ad la-Chasidut*, Tel Aviv 1984, 66–74.

25. See J. Greenstone, *The Messiah Idea*, 221 and 328 n. 19. Thus Shabbetai introduces himself e.g. as 'I the Lord your God, Shabbetai Zevi'. Down to the nineteenth century his followers referred to him with the honorific title ''Amirah', an abbreviation of *'Adonenu, Malkenu, yarum hodo'* (Our Lord, Our King, his Majesty be exalted) see Scholem, *Kabbalah*, 255.

26. For a brief discussion of this see P. Schäfer, 'Schabbati Zevi und die Sabbatianische Bewegung', *Emuna* V/VI, 1974, 341–2.

27. See Scholem, *Die jüdische Mystik*, 321–2, which states that the sacred ritual of transgression is the most characteristic feature of the Shabbetai movements.

28. See G. Scholem, *Be 'Iqbot ha-Mashiach*, Jerusalem 1944, 61, and see Schäfer, 'Schabbatai Zevi' (n. 23), 342, 344.

29. Cf. Scholem, *Die jüdische Mystik*, 342–3, 450 [n. 50], and his *The Messianic Idea*, 66ff., 344 n. 19.

30. Scholem, *The Messianic Idea*, 65–6, 147.

31. In going over to Islam Shabbetai was followed by the extremely antinomian Shabbetai Dunmeh sect, which was founded in Saloniki; its most radical wing was led by Barukhiah Russo.

Messianic Ideals in the German Reformation

Helga Robinson-Hammerstein

Messianism or millenarianism – the two terms are indeed often used interchangeably – is generally acknowledged to be a 'crisis cult', offering at crucial stages in history topical variants on the eschatological theme of the imminence of the Second Coming of Christ and the end of the existing order.[1] The crisis which engenders messianism appears to be marked by a dual disappointment in the material and spiritual sphere. There is no doubt that the development of the age of the Reformation, especially the period from 1500 to 1535 in Germany, is embedded in such a comprehensive sense of crisis and disorientation. Predictably it witnessed an intense popular as well as theological preoccupation with varying messianic expectations.[2] These prolific messianic expectations, however, are only very rarely adopted as the co-ordinating principle of interpretation in general histories of the German Reformation. The emphasis is placed instead on the analysis of events that testify to the comprehensive sense of crisis around 1500 and that resulted in the making of the Reformation in the 1520s and 1530s. Even topical and thematic treatments tend not to focus on the phenomenon of messianism and its role in shaping the Reformation, since this issue seems to belong to that limbo where social-cultural historians and ecclesiastical historians refuse to meet.[3]

There are essentially only two works, written under the immediate impact of the Nazi experience, which are specifically devoted to the formation and role of messianism in the Reformation and which have seminally influenced late twentieth-century evaluation of the phenomenon. Will-Erich Peuckert refers to his work *Die Grosse Wende* (first published in 1948), subtitled *Das Apokalyptische Saeculum und Martin*

Luther. Geistesgeschichte und Volkskunde as 'a child of pain and distress'.[4]
The underlying questions, as well as the general orientation, were
prompted by an inner urge to read the symbols and signs of the later
fifteenth and early sixteenth centuries. He perceived them as a mirror in
which fundamental truths of his own age, especially 1939–45, were
reflected: an age in which doom and gloom predominated and anxiety
generated improbable hopes.

The second book, which also had its distinctive fate of origin in the
revolutionary upheavals of the 1930s, has achieved a much wider
appreciation, particularly in the English-speaking world. Norman Cohn's
*Pursuit of the Millennium. Revolutionary Millenarians and Mystical
Anarchists of the Middle Ages*, first published in 1957, is still in print as a
paperback and graces the reading-lists for courses in early modern
history.[5] He assesses a critical selection of instances of apocalyptic
traditions from Jewish and early Christian times to the egalitarian
millenarianism and the messianic reign of John of Leyden in Münster in
1535, with a concluding treatment of the Free Spiriters in Oliver
Cromwell's England. His main findings are that 'revolutionary millenarianism flourishes only in certain specific social situations'. 'These *prophetae*
[of the millennium] found their following . . . where there existed an
unorganized, atomized population, rural or urban or both.'[6] Cohn seeks to
explain how the *prophetae* evolved over the centuries and to identify the
circumstances under which these leaders attracted previously disoriented
and disenchanted people into an improbable reality.

Leaving aside, for the moment, the messianism of the 'apocalyptic age'
as a crisis cult in the Peuckert-Cohn tradition, there is yet another, more
direct and spontaneous concern with the Messiah during the Reformation.
For if one interprets the core concern of the Lutheran Reformation in
Germany as a socio-intellectual phenomenon whose underlying propellant
was the redefinition of the God-man-relationship on the sole authority of
the Scriptures as the true Word of God, then the Messiah question poses
itself absolutely as a theological proposition. Applying humanist philological techniques to biblical analysis, this was Luther's inevitable
approach to the Messiah: a recovery of the early church's perception of the
Messiah as Christ the Redeemer (of which more will be said below).

It is the purpose of this article to ask which of these perceptions of the
Messiah, the traditional mediaeval or the scriptural one, shaped the
German Reformation. The straightforward answer should not be too
surprising: *both* perceptions were, of course, influential (if one can
simplify matters so far). However, it is not this predictable finding, but the

irreconcilable clash exemplified in the deadly contest between Martin Luther and Thomas Müntzer that contains the crucial truth about the forces that conditioned the German Reformation, as we shall see.

In the first instance, the following fact and its complex implications must be kept firmly in view: the German Reformation did not begin with Luther's theological *sola fide – sola scriptura – solus Christus* message. Reform was much talked about and many reforms were tried and abandoned in the course of the later fifteenth century.[7] In particular, the reform of the church in head and members came to nothing. Since hopes had been raised and dashed, popular discontent all the more readily expressed itself in terms of virulent anti-clericalism.[8] There is no doubt, however, that clerical members of the church were its severest and most trenchant critics. The church was the most obvious of all the institutions to criticize, since its *raison d'être* was so clearly defined and since its activities or lack of them impinged so crucially on people's vital interests and consciousness. However, while the period around 1500 was marked by verbal attacks on the church, an intense popular search for salvation was mounted: desperate though it was, it operated within the confines of the official church's penitential and sacramental systems.[9] The church was even able to keep the flock in check by its manipulation of the after-life (the sale of indulgences, the doctrine of purgatory), engendering an extreme form of anxiety which affected all social orders.[10] There was an explosion of popular religious activity, all designed to secure a better life hereafter if the individual did not succeed in extracting small survival-directed concessions for the life here and now: pilgrimages to new and old shrines, veneration of saints, but especially adulation of the Virgin as the most efficient intercessor.

On the socio-economic level all this could be contained and prevented from developing into attempts to overthrow society with the help of a popular leader. The blueprint of a scheme to deflect these problems effectively is the so-called *Reformatio Sigismundi*, originally written in 1438 but really coming into its own after 1480, when numerous printings disseminated its essentially conservative message.[11] This work, occasionally revised by later writers, cannot be placed in any existing millenarian tradition involving messianic leadership. It was an attempt to usher in a better age, to manipulate history through the revolution of a new order: an order which hinged essentially on the inner renewal, the moral rearmament of the people, as honest married folk. The premise on which the vision of the new order was elaborated was that the wrath of God is upon the people who have strayed like sheep without a shepherd. 'Obedience is dead, justice is grievously abused. Nothing stands in its proper order. Therefore God has withdrawn His grace from us.'[12] The tract culminates in the revelation of the new divinely willed order. This is worth quoting more fully, since it encapsulates many elements of later mediaeval messianism.

Be it known that it is God's will to have a new state and order come into being appropriate to the Christian faith. In the name of God and of the Lord Jesus Christ, we Sigismund, unworthy servant of God and Protector of the Holy Empire, make known what has been revealed to us, causing us much sadness in the thought of how small we are in the sight of God. . . . We affirm by our soul and by the passion of Our Lord Jesus Christ that what we are about to divulge was revealed to us in the year 1403 in Pressburg in Hungary. Toward dawn of Ascension Day, as the morning star appeared in the sky, a voice came to us saying: 'Sigismund arise, profess God and prepare a way for him who will come after you. He who will come after you is a priest through whom God will accomplish many things. He will be called Frederick of Lantneuen. He will raise the standard of the empire to the right of his own standard and between them he will raise a cross. He will rule sternly and with severity. No man shall be able to stand up against him. He will establish God's new order. . . .' From the very day on which we became the empire's servant we have striven with all our thoughts and efforts to establish and maintain the right order in Church and empire. We have reunited the papacy, convoked a council and brought order into the estate of holy Church. . . . However, the spiritual princes are opposed to the divine order. . . . Nothing can be completed until he arises whom God has chosen for the task. . . . Therefore when the time arrives and you hear of the coming of the appointed man, join this cause, help him to whom all wrongdoing is abhorrent. . . . His name shall be Frederick and he shall bring peace to the empire and all its lands and regions. . . . His work will go speedily. Though stern at first, his rule will grow mild; he may appear strange to us but will become familiar. Eternal life lies before us. Whoever craves it must join his cause. King and emperor do not admonish you: it is God, our Creator, who utters the prophecy. For the wicked hell is always open, but the faithful are called to heaven. Let us but bring order and obedience to our land and we shall soon overcome the heathens. This will happen. All men await his coming. The time is near. It shall be fulfilled.[13]

This obviously involved a considerable toning down of the notion of the expectation of the Emperor of the Last Days (*Endzeitkaiser*).[14] Folk-myths had kept the Sibylline prophecy alive and turned it into a target, clearly set but retreating. It was perceived as so harmless and non-volatile that the political admirers of Emperor Maximilian I (died 1519) attempted to harness this Frederick Redivivus myth to their sophisticated election campaign to identify Charles of Habsburg, Maximilian's grandson, as the divinely chosen Emperor of the Holy Roman Empire of the German Nation. They pointed out that he must be seen as the one promised in the old prophecies, since he was a man of the centre of the land, born in Ghent in the Netherlands, in the year of the 'semi-millennium', 1500, to which a great deal of significance was attached. Although it is true that the bribing of the seven electors (who had the sole power of choosing) was more effective in securing the election of Charles V, it is interesting to see what elements of the mediaeval messianic prophecies were considered sufficiently well known and worth using to generate a popular climate of support for the Habsburgs. Woodcut portraits of the 'young hero' were distributed with a caption. Relying on the mutually re-enforcing impact of text and image and vaguely promising better times to all people, it proclaimed: 'the cause will yet be won when Charles of noble house the son will take it for his own'.[15]

However, the *Reformatio Sigismundi* and its after-life reveals only the surface of the mental world inhabited by late mediaeval Germans. Its whole complexity is more fully displayed in a work which bundles together, with extraordinarily aggressive woodcut illustrations, all the doom predictions and apocalyptic visions on which contemporaries could and did draw: Johannes Lichtenberger's *Prognostic*, first published in Latin in 1488.[16] It is known from the many reprints in German translation or, more importantly, the profusion of partial reprints and adaptations in the *practicas* and horoscopes of the 1490s–1520s, how truly inspiring this work was. Its impact can most tellingly be traced in the flood of salacious pamphlets which utilized the prognostic set-pieces to announce to an already mightily agitated audience a second Flood for 1524, which would either destroy the whole world or destroy the reader's own community.[17] Lichtenberger's work was an accessible arsenal to stock the minds of ordinary people – addressed as 'the little people', the humble and meek of the Beatitudes – who had it read to them or heard it talked about. With its cloudy phrases that could easily be amplified and applied to specific events, and its doom-laden, anxiety-enhancing images of agonizing death and destruction, of the final battle, God's implacable wrath, Gog and Magog, the *pastor angelicus*, the sea-tossed ship of St Peter, *Fredericus redivivus* and a profusion of other graphic images besides, it fed the voracious appetites of contemporary Germans who had convinced themselves that they inhabited the doomed world of the Last Age.[18]

There is no scope here for a detailed investigation of the various elements of the eschatological prognostics of the imaginative twelfth-century systematizer, Abbot Joachim of Fiore, who embedded them in his trinitarian scheme of history as the Age of the Father (Old Testament), the Age of the Son (New Testament) and the Age of the Spirit. They have indeed been fully explored elsewhere.[19] Two points, however, need to be made to attest the powerful presence and influence of this prognostic tradition, carried forward by pseudo-Joachites to the threshold of the sixteenth century and beyond, on the mental world of the Germans of *circa* 1500. First, the prophecies in the prognostic tradition of Joachim of Fiore were linked to the forecasting evidence derived from the stars and planets (*astrologia iudiciaria*). The stellar arrangements were assumed to have been made entirely for the benefit of human society as a guide by which to regulate its affairs. The fusion of the two prognostic impulses forged a potent conjunction of impeccable authorities (*auctoritates*) that encapsulated irrefutable truths. Secondly, given the strong sense of popular piety around 1500, which was officially directed to focus attention on the Last Things and which produced a treacherous under-current of dreams and visions of the imminent end of the world, there can be no doubt that anxiety was increased by the prognostics. It is, however, equally true that such anxiety was deemed to be a beneficial conditioning factor to promote an inner renewal. Fear of punishment, so graphically displayed before their eyes, would make people wise and prompt them to change their lives of sin. Doom predictions could even be seen to contain an element of consolation. For while the texts and images announced that God was angry and was indeed bent on intensifying the already severe punishment so evident in the calamities of their present-day lives, suffering would finally end and a realm of peace and harmony begin. Fear in the later mediaeval prognostic tradition was indeed perceived as the seedbed in which the fruits of recovery and the ingredients of a better life would be nurtured.[20]

Albrecht Dürer's *Four Horsemen of the Apocalypse*, relentlessly locating the imminent destruction of the present order in the current age, conveys that same message of fear.[21] There is also a great deal of evidence to justify the conjecture that the representations of the Last Judgment which had been built into the very architecture of cathedrals (since the eleventh century), together with the whole economy of salvation from creation to the end,[22] assumed an intimidating, fear-inducing literal life of their own around 1500. All this prompted people to cling all the more tenaciously to the doom prognostics that appeared to offer at least some relief after unspeakable suffering.

It is difficult to say why these stirrings were not translated into more coherent actions of protest; but it is possible to argue that very special circumstances have to exist for anxiety to prompt action. Under most conditions anxiety seems to have an action-inhibiting, almost hypnotic effect. However, it is also true that no convincing messianic leader offered himself, who picked up these strands and co-ordinated them, together with the forces of material discontent, into a massive protest.[23] The potential was there; and this must be borne in mind when examining Luther's doctrine of the Messiah and the eschatological dimension of his theology.

Martin Luther's Messiah in the eschatological dimension of his theology

The following discussion can only offer some very general, and of necessity superficial observations, in stark contrast to the overwhelming wealth of studies which, however, defy brief summaries.

To begin with the obvious, Luther was a child of his times; the mental world in which he grew up was that of the late mediaeval messianic speculations sketched out above. That he shared the intense anxiety of his age, especially in respect of the question of justification, he confirmed in his autobiography.[24] However, he adopted the *sola scriptura* principle as the exclusively valid and secure authority on which to ground the discovery of the truth and by which to bring the practice and belief of the church into agreement with that of early Christianity. The exclusive adoption of this principle was automatically directed against many aspects of popular tradition (including late mediaeval prognostics) but especially against the ecclesiastical traditions on which the church based its claim to be the sole interpreter of Scripture.[25] Luther postulated for himself, and even for the laity, that God's Word was in the Scriptures, that no validation by any church was needed and that the Word in the New Testament meant the encounter of believers with the living Christ. He arrived at this uncompromising position as a result of the development of his distinctive humanist exegetical mode of working (*ad fontes*, to the sources). The process of the discarding of all other authorities has been carefully delineated by H. Junghans.[26] As in early Christendom, Jesus was the Messiah, the *Christos* of John 1.41 and 4.25, with all that this entailed about justification and law, sin and faith. Luther's message of salvation by faith in Christ alone offered a novel and utterly devastating challenge to everything that had developed as a belief-system within the mediaeval church. No compromise was possible. Luther's total intellectual break with the church and all it stood for has been stated in this way, although it is bound to remain controversial, in order to explain his absolutely unbending attitude towards the papal church as well as the Reformation radicals. This is how he saw his position himself and this determined his action.[27]

Luther's christology was eschatological in orientation, not because he might still have been caught up in the late mediaeval expectations, but as a result of his close reading of the Bible. The victory of Christ which has been achieved by death on the cross and his resurrection at Easter and which is effective in the faith of Christians in the present, will only become completely effective with Christ's Second Coming and the future *reunion* of Christ and his people. This bipolar eschatological dimension is already evident in Luther's *Lectures on Romans* 15.15–16. It is indeed a reworking of the dichotomous Pauline position on the resurrection of man here and now through faith and the resurrection on the Last Day'.[28]

Luther believed himself to be living in the Last Age before the Second Coming to which he fervently looked forward, encouraging his followers to do likewise and calling the final consummation 'the dear Last Day'. He utterly rejected the chiliasm of his day as misconceived in its prognostic calculations. He interpreted the millenium of Revelation 20 not according to tradition but as referring to an historic age starting in the past and ending with the papacy's becoming the sole manifestation of Antichrist. G. Seebass has argued that Luther became more and more convinced that the end was nigh, with his growing conviction that the pope was Antichrist.[29] This conception of Antichrist differs sharply from the traditional mediaeval one. For Luther the evidence that the pope was Antichrist was the fact that he fought against Christ's gospel of salvation, depriving people of the consolation of the gospel and replacing it with the doctrine of works and merits, which according to Daniel 11.36 and II Thessalonians 2.4 is the hallmark of the Antichrist.[30] In this way he also distinguished himself from the Hussite perception of the Antichrist: it was not the life of the church but its false teaching that demonstrated the true state of affairs. Luther gave this perception of Antichrist full reign in his vitriolic polemics of the 1540s. The more the true gospel is preached, the more the Antichrist rages in this world; but this is to be seen as a sign of the approaching end, because Christ's victory over the Antichrist is inevitable. This leads us back to Luther's definition of the Last Judgment as 'the dear Last Day', in complete contrast to the mediaeval *dies irae*. For Luther the

Judgment was a consummation devoutly to be wished, since it would finally reunite believers with the Messiah who has already redeemed them. The clear eschatological message of the New Testament had been overlaid, according to Luther, by the mediaeval church with false man-made traditions, which ultimately resulted in the doom-laden, anxiety-engendering predictions of the late Middle Ages.

From this same bipolar eschatological perspective Luther also fought against the manipulation of fear which he saw in operation in the salvation-system of the papal church. He argued strenuously and consistently that fear produced a false faith leading to an acceptance of false messiahs.[31] That some at least of his contemporaries appreciated the *sola fide* argument in that sense is shown by Albrecht Dürer's early response to Luther. He thanked Luther for freeing him from fear, in a letter which accompanied his dedication of a copy of his print, *Knight, Death and Devil*. A more far-reaching instance can be found in the manner in which the horrendous representations of the Last Judgment of the late Middle Ages ceased to figure in Lutheran churches. Lucas Cranach's depiction of the Old Faith (Protestant) and the New (man-made papal religion) is divided by the tree of Life. Salvation by faith is illustrated as the Christian man under the cross of Christ deriving the benefits of Christ's death and resurrection, represented by Christ's blood pouring over him. The representation of the man-made faith contains all the trappings of the papal church's manipulative system: Christ in judgment sitting on the rainbow; the tablets of the Law as the unfulfillable condition of justification by works; the Christian being pitchforked into the gaping mouth of hell by hideous devils.[32]

While Luther did not object to having himself represented as the returning Elijah or the Angel of Revelation 14.6 preceding the end of the world, his eschatological perspective also explains why he refused to be cast in the role of a 'reformer'. Only the gospel can bring about the Reformation: this effective Reformation is God's work; it will come to pass at the end of the present order.[33] The same bipolar eschatological perspective provides the context in which to appreciate the rationale behind Luther's 'Two Realms' theory, as two ideal constructs of the kingdom of this world, inhabited by sinners, totally separate from the Kingdom of God, inhabited by pure Christians. The kingdom of the world is the preliminary imperfect and unperfectible existence. The Kingdom of God is the one to which Christians aspire and where they will finally be united with Christ at the end of time. Luther conceived this as a *dynamic* construct.[34]

He severely castigated as false prophets and false messiahs those radicals who attempted to merge the two realms by displaying the most objectionable literalism and fundamentalism, which resulted in the use of force to constrain consciences. It was this reading of radical action which informed his harsh indictment of the Zwickau prophets and Andreas Karlstadt as agents of the Wittenberg Movement in 1521–2. It also explains the implacable severity with which he castigated the role of Thomas Müntzer in instigating rebellion and the actions of the Thuringian peasants in following him into an illusory society. This does not validate Luther's judgment of either event as a sustainable interpretation, even at the time; but it serves to characterize the nature of his eschatological thought in his consistent adherence to the Two Realms theory. His invariable arguments were that, firstly, man's nature was not perfectible and, secondly, the goal of spiritual perfection did not belong to the political realm, since it presupposed grace rather than power.[35]

Thomas Müntzer: messianic perceptions and revolutionary millenarianism

Thomas Müntzer's theological formation is still the subject of much debate: how 'Martinian' was he? Was he essentially a mystic or had he come under the influence of the Taborites, the main purveyors of radical millenialism? Without wishing to minimize the ingenious efforts at speculative reconstruction of his millenial revolutionary career, I must point out that these questions are more than usually futile, since so very little is known about Thomas Müntzer's early life before he came to Zwickau in 1520.[36] The problem lies not so much in early influences as in the later utilization and integration of the millenial currents that ran across central Europe. There is no doubt, however, that first and foremost, judging from the records of his early sermons, he was conversant with the humanist philological technique of biblical exegesis. While he was intellectually in sympathy with the mystical spiritualism of Johann Tauler, it appears that he adopted the humanist critique and discarded the whole scholastic apparatus of theological scholarship quite independently of Luther.[37] Like Luther, Thomas Müntzer was not very systematic in his approach to theological, or for that matter, political questions. He was a thinker whose thoughts were refined in the crucible of historical events, the significance of which he interpreted quite differently from Luther. There can be no question that he was a highly learned scholar, a consummate intellectual, whose close encounter with the biblical texts prompted questions that challenged the canon of assumptions within the Catholic Church. His preoccupation with Christ's passion and its meaning, his appreciation of the church's inability to point the way to true salvation, show a close affinity to Luther. In an early letter to Luther he signed himself in fact, 'Thomas Müntzer whom you have brought to birth by the Gospel'.[38]

Thomas Müntzer's millennial process of radicalization first revealed itself in the following problematic over which Luther agonized just as much as Müntzer, but with fundamentally different results. Luther, who had made the Word of God the basis of the Reformation (increasingly under the outward constraining protection of existing secular authorities), did indeed ask himself, like Müntzer, why it was that the proclamation of the Word did not change people's lives. If the Word was all-powerful, if it was *the* creative energy that linked man with God, then why did the recipients of its message remain such unredeemed sinners; why did they not start to build a God-fearing, peaceful, harmonious society? To Luther the answer was ultimately obvious, viewed from the eschatological perspective sketched out above. The more the pure gospel was preached, the more the devil (and his Antichrist) raged against it and stopped up people's spiritual ears against it. Furthermore, in accordance with the strict separation of the Two Realms, the kingdom of this world was bound to remain imperfectible and spiritual salvation could not be achieved by forcing consciences or by rebellion. (The latter only became fully clear to him as a result of Müntzer's actions in the Thuringian Peasants' War.)

To Müntzer this answer was too facile. Man who had been enlightened by the Word of God must act out the will of God in this world, if necessary by changing the prevailing socio-economic realities which alienated him from God. The watchword 'freedom of the Christian' meant for Luther the active sustaining of the tension caused by belonging to both of the Two Realms. For Müntzer it meant the active – eventually forceful – removal of everything that he perceived as hindering life in true faith, regardless of social status.

In the course of his Zwickau experience it became clear to Müntzer that theory and practice must become one to fulfil the will of God urgently: to realize his kingdom on earth. Müntzer found Luther's separation of the two kingdoms not only theologically unsound but also intellectually dishonest: the easy way out adopted by the 'soft-living flesh of Wittenberg'. Luther needed the protection of princes and was prepared to abandon the prescribed – as Müntzer read it – Christianization of the world for the sake of the preservation of the existing alienating social order.

Thomas Müntzer's progressive millennial radicalization was his response to socio-political circumstances which he encountered or which can be traced to the main stages of his missionary wanderings from Zwickau to Prague, to Allstedt, to Mühlhausen and eventually to Frankenhausen. Moving further and further away from the acceptance of existing reality (also in the sense of losing his mental grip on reality), Müntzer interpreted the conditioning which he observed around him invariably from the perspective of the necessary and urgent realization of the will of God: that is, the categorical imperative of the Christianization of the kingdom of this world. In respect of the Word by which God's will was communicated, he shifted to a mystical position as he faced social realities which he encountered as hindering the realization of the will of God. He adopted the notion of the 'everlasting Word' which must reach men's hearts. God himself will speak it directly into men's hearts through the Holy Spirit. God's Word must be *experienced*. It can only be experienced through suffering, which turns the heart into a receptive vessel of the Spirit. Whereas it can be said of Luther that his mode of thinking predisposed him to frame questions so that there could be biblical answers, Müntzer resorted to visions and portents rather than adhering to biblical texts to attempt the Christianization of the world.[39]

In the rationalization of his responses to changing human conditions as he encountered them, Müntzer drew on millennial traditions of the later Middle Ages which he found alive and active among the people for whom he felt responsible as pastor. This process of assimilation can clearly be seen in operation when Müntzer established contact with the secret brotherhood of impoverished weavers at Zwickau. With their emphasis on dreams and visions they showed him the hitherto blocked access to the Christianization of the world. With their secret brotherhood organization they provided him with the beginnings of a workable model for its realization.[40] When his Allstedt ministry witnessed the establishment of the League of the Elect, and his Mühlhausen activities resulted in the Eternal League of God, he had moved further on the path of radicalization. This development was always in response to circumstances as he experienced them in the light of Taborite chiliasm, with which he had forged a conscious link in Prague.[41]

It is not the purpose of this discussion to explore in detail all the stages of Müntzer's career as a revolutionary millennialist: the purpose is rather to suggest that this career evolved quite logically. Once he had posed the question of how the urgent Christianization of the world could be brought about, having dismissed Luther's separation of the two kingdoms, he became prone to influences of Taborite millennialism. The transition from a passively apocalyptic reading of events to an active and violent intervention followed the same impeccable logic. The cleansing of Christianity could not simply be achieved by forming model communities of the elect, who quietly enjoyed their lives in the conviction that they had been singled out. They must act; and their Christianizing action must result in the destruction of sinners by violence and rebellion. Müntzer's growing sense of apocalyptic mission can be traced in the titles which he adopted in signing his letters. In his other writings too he variously referred to himself as 'messenger of Christ',[42] 'a son of shaking (Job 38) to the impious',[43] 'a willing courier of God',[44] 'a disturber of the un-believers',[45] 'servant of the elect of God',[46] 'a servant of God against the godless',[47] 'Thomas Müntzer, with the sword of Gideon'[48] and the new Daniel.

The necessity of violence is rationalized and justified by a topical interpretation of the Second Book of Daniel in the *Sermon to the Saxon Princes*.[49] Thomas Müntzer's exegesis presents his mature revolutionary millennialism which relies on an elect human agency to exercise God's wrath. In true apocalyptic expectation he was convinced that he and his followers would be spared this wrath, since God was pleased with them for doing His work by violently cleansing Christian society. With this assurance Müntzer encouraged his peasant followers when they were facing the overwhelming military might of the princes.

> Even if there are only three of you whose trust in God is unperturbable and who seek His name and honour alone, you have no fear of a hundred thousand. So go to it, go to it, go to it! The time has come, the evil-doers are running like scared dogs! Alert the brothers, so that they may be at peace and testify to their conversion. It is absolutely crucial – absolutely necessary! Go to it, go to it, go to it! Show no pity, even though Esau suggest kind words to you, Genesis 33. Pay no attention to the cries of the godless. They will entreat you ever so warmly, they will whimper and wheedle like children. Show no pity, as God has commanded in the words of Moses, Deuteronomy 7; and he has revealed the same thing to us too. Alert the villages and towns and especially the mineworkers and other good fellows who will be of use. We cannot slumber any longer.[50]

Luther interpreted the outcome of the battle of Frankenhausen as the vanquishing of Müntzer's brand of messianism and the victory of his own messianic perception.[51] The Reformation in Germany was shaped by the conflict of these two forms of messianism.

Notes

1. See entry 'Messianismus' in *RGG*[3], vol. IV, 895–900.
2. The sense of crisis and the different interpretations of the phenomenon are well summarized in Rainer Wohlfeil, *Einführung in die Geschichte der deutschen Reformation*, Munich 1982, 18, 46ff.
3. Euan Cameron, *The European Reformation*, Oxford 1991, shows a greater interest in these questions.
4. Will-Erich Peuckert, *Die Grosse Wende*, Darmstadt 1966, 647.
5. Norman Cohn, *The Pursuit of the Millenium. Revolutionary Millenarians and Mystical Anarchists in the Middle Ages*, London 1957, revised 1961 and 1970 (1970 edition used here).
6. Cohn (n. 5), 281–2.
7. For various attempts at 'reform from within' see Cameron (n. 3), 38ff.
8. Hans-Jürgen Goertz, 'Aufstand gegen die Priester. Antiklerikalismus und reformatorische Bewegungen', in Peter Blickle (ed.), *Bauer, Reich und Reformation*, Stuttgart 1982, 182–209; Gerald Strauss (ed.), *Manifestations of Discontent on the Eve of the Reformation*. Bloomington, Indiana 1971.
9. Willy Andreas, *Deutschland vor der Reformation*, Berlin [7]1972, offers a vivid picture of this frenetic search for salvation. Bernd Boeller, 'Piety in Germany around 1500', in Gerald Strauss, *Pre-Reformation Germany*, London 1972, 13–42, is the most frequently cited review of available evidence. See also William E. Monter, *Ritual, Myth and Magic in Early Modern Europe* (Chapter 1), Brighton 1983; P. Baumgart, 'Formen der Volksfrömmigkeit: Krise der alten Kirche und der reformatorischen Bewegungen', in Peter Blickle (ed.), *Revolte und Revolution in Europa, HZ* NF, Beiheft 4, 1975, 196ff.
10. See William Bouwsma, 'Anxiety and the Formation of Early Modern Culture', now in id., *A Usable Past. Essays in European Cultural History*, Berkeley, Los Angeles and Oxford 1990, 157–89.
11. Lother Graf zu Dohna, *Reformatio Sigismundi. Beiträge zum Verständnis einer Reformschrift des 15. Jahrhunderts*, Göttingen 1960.
12. Strauss, *Manifestations* (n. 8), 4 (printed in Heinrich Koller, ed., *Reformation Kaiser Sigismunds*, Stuttgart 1964, MGH, Staatsschriften des späteren Mittelalters, IV).
13. Strauss, *Manifestations* (n. 8), 30–1.
14. Cohyn (n. 5), 71ff. and 108ff.; Peuckert (n. 4), 213ff.
15. Karl Brandi, *The Emperor Charles V* (ET by C. V. Wedgwood, 1937), London 1967, 109: 'Ich hoff, die Sach soll werden gut, So Carolus, des edel Plut, die Sach tut fur sich nehmen.'
16. Dietrich Kurse, *Johannes Lichtenberger. Eine Studie zur Geschichte der Prophetie und Astrologie*, Lübeck-Hamburg 1960. Lichtenberger's *Pronostication in Latino* was first published in Heidelberg by Heinrich Knoblochtzer in 1488. Cf. in general Marjorie Reeves, *Prophecy in the Later Middle Ages*, Oxford 1969.
17. H. Robinson-Hammerstein, 'The Battle of the Booklets: Prognostic Tradition and Proclamation of the Word in Early Sixteenth-Century Germany', in Paola Zambelli (ed.), *Astrologi Hallucinati: Stars and the End of the World in Luther's Time*, Berlin 1986.

18. See n. 17 and in greater detail Will-Erich Peuckert (n. 4).

19. See n. 16 and entry 'Eschatologie', TRE X, 1982, 305–14; D. C. West (ed.), *Joachim of Fiore in Christian Thought. Essays on the Influence of the Calabrian Prophet*, New York 1975.

20. Bernard McGinn (ed.), *Visions of the End*, New York 1979.

21. Andreas (n. 9), 181ff.

22. Andreas (n. 9), 18.

23. Very important in this context: E. Lerner, 'Medieval Prophecy and Religious Dissent', in *Past and Present* 72, 1976, 3–24; M. Reeves, *Joachim of Fiore and the Prophetic Future*, London 1976.

24. Bernhard Lohse, *Martin Luther. An Introduction to his Life and Writings*, Philadelphia 1986; Walther von Loewenich, *Martin Luther. The Man and his Work*. Minneapolis 1986, are just two examples.

25. On the two types of tradition see Heiko A. Oberman, 'Quo Vadis Petre? Tradition from Irenaeus to Humani Generis', in id. (ed.), *The Dawn of the Reformation. Essays in Late Medieval and Early Reformation Thought*, Edinburgh 1986, 269–96.

26. Helmar Junghans, *Der junge Luther und die Humanisten*, Göttingen 1985.

27. A useful discussion of Luther's self-perception can be found in Cameron (n. 3), 111, 192.

28. An assessment of this dual eschatology is most readily available in TRE X, 310ff.

29. See the brief sketch by Gottfried Seebass in TRE III, 1978, entry 'Apokalypse'. He provides the evidence, but I have somewhat departed from his interpretation. Seebass also points to Luther's acceptance of Johann Carion's computation of three Ages in Luther's *Supputatio*, 1541.

30. H. Pruess, *Die Vorstellungen vom Antichrist*, 1960, and a very useful brief synopsis in Paul Althaus, *Die Theologie Martin Luthers*, Gütersloh [6]1983.

31. See my edition of Heinrich Pastoris, *Casting a German Horoscope*, Dublin 1980.

32. These are my own observations based on an examination of the altarpieces of Lucas Cranach the Elder and Lucas Cranach the Younger.

33. Heiko A. Oberman, 'Martin Luther – Vorläufer der Reformation', in *Verifikationen. Festschrift für Gerhard Ebeling zum 70. Geburtstag*, ed. E. Jüngel, J. Wallmann and W. Werbeck, Tübingen 1982, 91–119.

34. J. M. Potter, 'Luther and Political Millenarianism: The Case of the Peasants' War', *Journal of the History of Ideas* 42, 1981, 389–406. Potter makes some very perceptive observations on Luther's use of language and the linguistic shortcomings of his opponents in this context. See also Gerhard Ebeling, *Luther. Einführung in sein Denken*, Tübingen [4]1981, reprinted 1990, 200ff., 225.

35. See Potter (n. 34). Luther's indictment of Müntzer is more fully presented by Carl Hinrichs, *Luther und Müntzer. Ihre Auseinandersetzung über Obrigkeit und Widerstandsrecht*, Arbeiten zur Kirchengeschichte XXIX, Berlin [2]1962.

36. Hans-Jürgen Goertz, *Innere und äussere Ordnung in der Theologie Thomas Müntzers*, Studies in the History of Christian Thought II, Leiden 1967. Very important recent publications are: Tom Scott, *Thomas Müntzer*, Houndsmill 1989; Abraham Friesen, *Thomas Müntzer. A Destroyer of the Godless. The Making of a Sixteenth-Century Revolutionary*, Berkeley 1990; Peter Matheson (ed.), *The Collected Works of Thomas Müntzer*, Edinburgh 1988.

37. Scott (n. 36), 11.

38. See Matheson (n. 36), 18–22.

39. J. M. Potter (n. 34), 400, and most importantly Reinhard Schwarz, *Die apokalyptische Theologie Thomas Müntzers und der Taboriten*, Tübingen 1977.

40. Scott (n. 36), 24.

41. Schwarz (n. 39), 56ff., 79ff., 93ff.

42. Matheson (n. 36), 46.

43. Ibid., 51.

44. Ibid., 54.

45. Ibid., 67.

46. Ibid., 82.

47. Ibid., 142.

48. Ibid., 151, 156, 157.

49. Ibid., 236ff.

50. Scott (n. 36), 153.

51. A consideration of the community experiments of the peaceful (notably in Bohemia and Moravia) and the militant (Münster 1535) Anabaptists – which could not be included here for lack of space – would have further demonstrated the range of millennialism in the German Reformation.

III · Some Contemporary Implications

Marx's Messianic Faith

Alistair Kee

'Send us no more messiahs,' was the heartfelt cry of D. H. Lawrence. We who stand now reviewing the course of the twentieth century know exactly what he meant. The message is clear: there have been too many false messiahs. They have misled and confused ordinary people into forsaking the one true Messiah. Or rather is the message not entirely the opposite? Has not the possibility of confusion arisen precisely because Christ has too long been pictured in these very same terms as these false saviours? Are those irreligious movements of modern times to be stridently rejected as alien voices, or rather do they not come as unwitting messengers to a church that has gone its own way? And in the modern world there is no more significant message than that of original and authentic Marxism. Indeed the sweeping away in 1989 of what Marx himself referred to as 'crude and unreflective communism'[1] has made it possible for us to attend more carefully and urgently to that Voice within the voice.

Is Marxism but a secular form of the Christian religion, or rather did Marxism arise with the rediscovery of those revolutionary elements in early Christianity long since thankfully set by aside by the rulers of this world and their obedient house chaplains? Is Marxism a distorted version of a messianic movement, or rather is it the true form of that ancient tradition beside which Christian messianism is a degraded perversion? Has Marxism set its face resolutely against God's Messiah, or rather has it not focused single-mindedly upon the Kingdom of Righteousness in contrast to a Christian image of the Messiah which is fundamentally fascist?

When invited to write this article I was asked to focus attention on possible messianic elements within Marxism. How shall we approach this question? Shall we immediately reduce the issue to the question: Was Karl Marx a messianic figure? Or, in parallel to the Jesus research shall we ask the more erudite question whether Marx thought of himself as a messiah? No, we shall certainly not begin with such questions, to which in any case the answer is a resounding No. Marx, a messianic figure! This self-styled 'bourgeois ideologist', who thought he had betrayed his class? How could he have betrayed it, since born into the middle class he married into the aristocracy; since in order to avoid the distraction of work he accepted money derived from the exploitation of Manchester mill-workers. A messianic figure? This man who was never seen in public without his monocle and frock coat? A messianic revolutionary leader of the masses? This man, perhaps the only man in history to hold a certificate from a German court proclaiming him entirely innocent of any influence whatever in the proletarian uprising of Köln? No, Karl Marx could not have been mistaken for a messianic figure. Nor did he ever display for a moment that megalomania characteristic of Fascist messiahs. However, if we yielded to the insistent demand that we give him a historical title, a title which he never espoused and at which he would have scoffed, then he would not be the messiah, but John the Baptist. He was not the one to bring the history of oppression to an end, but like that uncomfortable figure of old he knew in which direction to point.

No, we cannot answer the question by looking at the person or life of Marx. Perhaps we could approach it by comparing the pseudo-messianism of Marxism with its true expressions in Judaism and Christianity. Unfortunately it may transpire that Marxism alone is the truly messianic movement. As we shall see, early Marxism is nothing but the messianic proclamation of the imminent coming of the age of justice and peace. That is not the issue. The issue is rather to what extent classical Judaism and orthodox Christianity are really characterized by messianism at all? Is Marxism a messianic movement? Who cares? Much more important is the question whether the messianic element in Marxism challenges and corrects the assumptions about the Messiah within religious thought and practice. I wish to draw attention to three features of Marxism which are relevant to this matter.

1. The redemption of our time and place

The earliest influences on our lives are often the most profound and abiding. So it was with Marx: Judaism, Christianity and Hegel in that order. Everything else took its place within premises taken over from these three closely related systems. Hegel considered himself a good Lutheran, and Marx till the end of his life avowed himself 'a pupil of that mighty thinker' whose genius first uncovered the laws of historical motion. It would be absurd to look for historical materialism in the earliest thoughts of Marx, but let us not think for a moment that his developed system was raised up on any other foundations than the Judaeo-Christian heritage which was so formative on him in his youth. Karl Marx came from a family which on both sides could trace its history back several centuries to Poland and Hungary and many of his ancestors were distinguished Jewish rabbis. It is normal to dismiss this as a chance of birth and to assume that his personal atheism meant that he broke with the Jewish community and its traditions. That this is not so can be seen for example in a remark Marx made in a letter to Arnold Ruge. In 1843 the Jews of Köln wished to present a petition to the Provincial Assembly, and the head of the Jewish community approached Marx, requesting him to write it for them. This he agreed to do. As is well known, his father, a prominent lawyer in Trier, felt compelled by antisemitic Prussian laws to become a member of the Lutheran church. No religious conversion was involved. Karl was enrolled in the Gymnasium, which had formerly been a Jesuit college. The most important premises of Marx's whole philosophy derive from this religious background, a fact which is easily demonstrated from an examination of his schoolboy essays.

Few of us would welcome Marx's fate in having scholars scrutinize his schoolboy essays and his school-leaving certificate, a document which with some prescience declared him to have a sound understanding of religion, but a poor grasp of history. Of interest to our particular subject is the German essay, entitled 'Reflections of A Young Man on the Choice of a Career'. Marx was to become an outstanding student and one of the best critical minds of his century. He could have turned his abilities to his own advantage, yet from his schoolboy days he exhibited a dedication to using his gifts in the service of others less fortunate.

> Religion itself teaches us that the ideal being whom all strive to copy sacrificed himself for the sake of mankind, and who would dare to set at nought such judgments? If we have chosen the position in life in which we can most of all work for mankind, no burdens can bow us down, because they are sacrifices for the benefit of all; then we shall experience no petty, limited, selfish joy, but our happiness will belong to millions, our deeds live on quietly perpetually at work.

For Marx, the life of self-sacrifice for the good of others follows from the example of the sacrifice of Christ, an example which he was to follow for the rest of his life, at great personal cost to himself and subsequently at great suffering to his wife and children. But this was not simply a view of Christ as a moral example. He also wrote an exegetical essay on the subject of 'The Union of Believers with Christ According to John 15.1–14, Showing its Basis and Essence, Its Absolute Necessity, and its Effects'. The young Marx tells us that 'man cannot by himself achieve the purpose for which God brought him into being out of nothing'. Anyone who has achieved union with Christ can bear the blows of the world, 'for who can oppress him, who could rob him of his Redeemer?' By the time Marx came to write his doctoral dissertation he had adopted the 'brusque, dictatorial, atheistic and republican tone' of the Doctors' Club, but he did not depart from the premises of his early religious position, as we shall presently observe.

One of the central themes in Marx's early writings was freedom, emancipation from various mechanisms of social control, in particular emancipation from injustice and oppression. The status of serf was abolished in Prussia only a decade before the birth of Marx. His parents had suffered from oppressive racial laws. Several of Marx's friends were persecuted because of their criticisms of religion, notably his mentor Bruno Bauer. Strict censorship laws led to the closure of journals, including the *Rheinische Zeitung* which Marx edited. When in 1844 he finally left Germany for France it was for the sake of freedom of expression. Soon, living among the Paris communards, he was to turn his attention to liberation from the oppressive conditions of the alienated and dehumanizing labour characteristic of the emerging capitalist economy. It is therefore not surprising that as Marx clarified his thought by dealing with Hegel's *Rechtsphilosophie* he should finally ask this question: 'Where, then, is the *positive* possibility of a German emancipation?'

Before examining his answer it is necessary to provide a context. During this time the most influential of the Young Hegelians, the left-wing critics of the master, was Ludwig Feuerbach, whose name is remembered now for his projection theory of religion. According to Feuerbach man projects his hopes, fears and values on to God. Religion therefore tells us little about a divine being over against man: it tells us a great deal about society at that stage in its development. As he observes in *The Essence of Christianity*, 'the measure of thy God is the measure of thy understanding'. The divine attributes are therefore in reality human attributes, selected and projected unconsciously. But since the divine attributes are clearly not attributes of individuals, Feuerbach brings forward a more appropriate subject. 'All divine attributes, all attributes which make God God, are attributes of the species . . .' By this means Feuerbach preserved the values associated with

God, but he sought to avoid the unreality of idealism (and theology) by applying these divine predicates to a subject within human, material history. I have taken time to mention all this, since Marx not only accepted this projection view of religion, but made it the starting point for his own critical philosophy, expanding its application from religion to the criticism of the state, philosophy, money, alienated labour and private property. But we can now return to Marx's question, 'Where, then, is the positive possibility of a German emancipation?'

After his essentially negative criticism of these elements in contemporary society Marx now seeks a positive way forward to emancipation. Injustice and oppression exist in society and Marx has now dedicated his life to exposing them. Observation led him to reject the assurances implied in Hegel's claim that 'the real is rational'. The real for those suffering under the conditions of modern capitalist society was anything but rational. But this negative criticism could not of itself liberate. Of course it was possible that a revolution could take place in which the oppressors would be replaced by the oppressed. But such an Orwellian revolution would merely perpetuate suffering and oppression. Now living in France, Marx formed a view of history as a sequence of class struggles. Each new class which arises takes over political and economic power, and prevents the older classes continuing to oppress it. But in this sequence the new class eventually oppresses those beneath it. This was still not the positive development for which Marx looked. What was required was yet another class, but now the last class, which with its coming would not only end its oppression, but would not initiate new forms of oppression.

> A class must be formed which has *radical chains*, a class in civil society which is not a class of civil society, a class which is the dissolution of all classes, a sphere of society which has a universal character because its sufferings are universal, and which does not claim a *particular redress* because the wrong which is done to it is not a *particular wrong* but *wrong in general*. There must be formed a sphere of society which claims no *traditional* status, but only a human status, a sphere which is not opposed to particular consequences, but is totally opposed to the assumptions of the German point of view.

In seeking liberation Marx envisages not an existing social class, but a class which will be of such a character that it will be able to act in a new way. This new Subject will be able to perform a new Work. The quotation continues as he describes:

a sphere, finally, which cannot emancipate itself without emancipating itself from all the other spheres of society, which is, in short, a *total loss of humanity* and which can only redeem itself by *a total redemption of humanity*, this dissolution of society, as a particular class, is the *proletariat*.

The Young Hegelians in their criticism of idealism assumed that they must be materialists, but there is no trace of empirical observation in this passage. Marx is not describing any existing social class, not even the new industrial working class. However, it is not difficult to identify the source of his vision of liberation. Feuerbach took the attributes of God and projected them on to the human species, or rather on to a non-existent ideal social Subject. Now Marx takes the attributes of Christ and projects them onto a non-existing ideal social Subject. From Christian doctrine he applies this truth that the Person and the Work are one. Oppression cannot be ended by the oppressors, just as the power of evil cannot be defeated by the wrongdoer. The liberation of mankind can be brought about only by the appearance of one who is oppressed but will not become an oppressor, one who is wronged but will not use the power of evil to attempt to overcome that wrong. This is what Marx means by redemption.

Inevitably most theological terms were originally borrowed from secular language. When first used they would have considerable power of communication for this reason. The corollary is that when they are retained beyond their use in common speech they become specifically theological and lose this power. However, a movement in the opposite direction can also happen, when profound dimensions of secular events or movements can only be designated through a re-appropriation of theological terms. This is what has happened in this passage. In the ancient world the term *apolutrosis* (redemption) was a secular word from the market place. It referred, for example, to the buying back of a slave. The unfortunate, who could not save himself, would be liberated by someone acting on his behalf. It was therefore a powerful image when applied in the New Testament to the work of Christ. Thus Paul says that 'since all have sinned and fall short of the glory of God, they are justified by his grace as a gift, through the redemption which is in Christ Jesus . . .' (Romans 3.23–4). 'In him we have redemption through his blood . . .' (Ephesians 1.7). In both of these passages Luther translated *apolutrosis* with the word *Erlösung*. Not that Marx uses this word. He uses *Wiedergewinnung*. It is a secular word, as were *Erlösung* and *apolutrosis* originally. It means 'recovery' or 'reclamation'. But as I have just observed, there are occasions when the profound dimensions of a secular movement require the use of theological terms. For this reason I have given the English translation provided by the distinguished Marx scholar Tom Bottomore. He bites the bullet and translates *Wiedergewinnung* as 'redemption', which is exactly what Marx means.

But is this an empoverished, humanistic understanding of the redemption which is required in history if liberation is to be realized? On the contrary, it provides a powerful challenge to that tendency within Christianity which has gladly translated the work, and hence the person of Christ into a metaphysical and idealistic sphere, entirely unrelated to the historical, the material and the human sphere. As we saw from his schoolboy essay, Marx understood very well that this redemption, this emancipation of the captive, this liberation of the oppressed, was not something that could be brought about simply by determined human actions. For this reason he sees what is required, but does not fall into the easy optimism of claiming that the working class or any class can perform the necessary work. Something else is required, beyond human effort, and this constitutes the second of the elements in Marx's messianic philosophy which challenges Christian doctrine and practice.

2. The moral goal of history

In the Gospel of John and in theology of the Alexandrian School Christ is the Logos, the creative Word of God. Or as Pascal was later to put it: 'Christ is the Reason of all things'. In a truly messianic theology Christ does not simply act in another sphere. He is the internal logic, the inner fabric of the whole of human history. But has that been a feature of Christian theology throughout the centuries? Scholars of the salvation-history school were able to trace with great confidence the mighty acts of God in history from creation to the resurrection. And then silence. In what sense is Christ now the inner logic and the very fabric of continuing world history, leading not to the end of history but the goal of history? And yet no matter how silent the theologians are on this matter, the inner logic and very fabric of history, the goal towards which all history is moving, is the second striking characteristic of Marx's messianic philosophy.

Those who are immersed in Western culture may think that ideas about a goal of history, or history having a linear and meaningful development, are the common property of religious and non-religious thinkers. This is not so. A cyclical view of history is not only the common view of the great cultures of India and China, but more closely corresponds to experience

and observation. The cyclical is the experience of ovulation and menstrua-
tion. It is the universal pattern of the seasonal year. It could well be the
pattern of the whole cosmos from explosion to implosion. No, the linear
view of meaningful history, history proceeding towards a goal, is anything
but natural. It derives from religion, even when it is taken over by secular
thinkers. Indeed this was Nietzsche's criticism of those who halted
between two ways, those who had set aside the religious beliefs which in
fact provide the foundations of Western thought and culture. Nietzsche
saw clearly that those who lay aside the foundations have no right to
appropriate what previously rested upon them. Thus in his 'revaluation of
all values' he claimed that 'the goal of humanity cannot lie in the end but
only in its highest specimens'. With great courage and consistency he
relinquished all claim to teleology, and turned instead to the alternative:
eternal recurrence. Marx experienced no such alienation from Christian
morality and teleology. He was able to continue within this occidental
frame of reference because the religious model had been appropriated by
philosophy. In Hegel's *Phenomenology* nothing is merely observed:
everything is deduced. In the Preface to the Second Edition of *Capital*,
Marx acknowledges the genius of the master.

> The mystification which the dialectic suffers in Hegel's hands by no
> means prevents him from being the first to present its general forms of
> motion in a comprehensive and conscious manner. With him it is
> standing on its head. It must be inverted, in order to discover the
> rational kernel within the mystical shell.

The proposition that history is proceeding inexorably towards a moral goal
does not arise from observation of the world around us. Hegel took the idea
from the doctrine of providence, but in his system the dynamic was
internalized. It is no longer the transcendent God manipulating history so
that his will is done. Rather it is Reason which now works immanently
within history, its internal logic, its inner fabric. Marx's historical
materialism is but the materialization of the Hegelian view of history. To
claim that there is a material principle guiding human history was of course
an outrage to Hegel's loyal followers, but that in-house dispute should not
disguise from us the fact that the all-important premise on which historical
materialism is based came to Marx from Hegel, just as it came to that good
Lutheran from biblical religion.

In the Bible there is a series of dispensations. Hegel traced a series of
stages: consciousness, self-consciousness, reason, spirit and religion.
Marx, in a well known passage, suddenly uncovers a completely different

account of history, one which begins neither with divine nor with spiritual causes.

In broad outline Asiatic, ancient feudal, and modern bourgeois modes of production can be designated as progressive epochs in the economic formation of society.

History is guided and governed by a series of modes of production, which each in its own epoch forms the material base upon which the institutional superstructure of society is raised up. For Marx these epochs are progressive, not simply in material terms such as economic efficiency. They are progressive also in moral terms, marking a stage in the process of the development of the truly human life, the realization of human potential. But there is one further point, a premise which was also taken from Hegel. According to Hegel's dialectical view of history conflicts and contradictions may seem negative, but they have the positive effect of leading to an outcome which could not otherwise be achieved. No crumb falls from his table: each event contributes to the complex whole. *Hic Rhodus: hic saltus* – which obscurely Hegel took to mean, you cannot jump over your time and place. The higher stages of history require the earlier. When Marx took over this premise he claimed that for example it is not possible to move directly from feudalism to socialism. Every society must go through the capitalist stage. Capitalism for Marx was the most radical and the most humanizing revolution the world had hitherto seen. Speaking of modern industrial society he claimed in the *Communist Manifesto* that capitalism 'has thus rescued a considerable part of the population from the idiocy of the rural life'. Capitalism cannot be ignored, or circumvented: like everything else in the Hegelian world-view, it must be superseded.

Marx therefore claimed to have discovered the true basis of the development of human history. In common with religion and philosophy he believed that history was not directed by the will or intention of men. It is for this reason that Marxism is referred to as being 'scientific'. In the Preface to *Capital* Marx refers to 'the natural laws of capitalist production', 'working themselves out with iron necessity'. In the Preface to the English edition of the *Communist Manifesto* Engels makes this extraordinary claim, namely, that historical materialism 'is destined to do for history what Darwin's theory has done for biology', a view which Marx first expressed in a letter to Engels soon after reading Darwin's book in 1860. According to Marx, therefore, there is a force within history, directing its course towards a moral and humanizing goal, but although men participate in the process, its course is determined by iron necessity, quite independent of their will or intention. This is a truly messianic philosophy of history. Although based on premises drawn from religion, it makes claims which go far beyond the most creative or courageous theologians. As such it constitutes the second challenge of Marx to the claims of those who follow Christ. Is human history demonstrably moving in a moral direction towards the realization of full humanity for all? And if not, is religion anything more than pie in the sky? Who today is prepared to put his hand up and say what God is doing in the contemporary world? And if no answer can be given, is this the same faith as that of Jesus and his earliest followers? With this question about faith, we come to the third and final challenge of Marx's messianic philosophy. Marx was a proclaimer of good news to the poor. Why have so many taken courage from his words rather than the words of those proclaiming faith in Christ?

3. Justice triumphs in history

Although Marx rather pretentiously drew a parallel between his theory of historical materialism and Darwin's theory of evolution he was no scientist. Of course it would be possible to form an intuition of such a development in history, and to seek to establish or disprove it through painstaking examination of the relevant empirical economic data. But Marx was neither equipped nor motivated to perform such a tedious task. In a review of Marx's *Contribution to a Critique of Political Economy* Engels assures us that Marx could have proceeded 'historically or logically', and chose the latter as being 'the most suitable'. We know better. Historical materialism comes from religion and philosophy, from 'logic' and certainly not from a scientific study of the data, from 'history'. Marx could not be satisfied with merely material issues. From his schoolboy days he was motivated by a righteous desire to expose and thereby oppose injustice and oppression. Ironically, if historical materialism had been established as a scientific law he would not have been interested in it. His only interest in such a law was if it demonstrated that history was moving towards a moral goal, that the kingdom of justice would be established – necessarily and inexorably. From this two issues arise.

The first concerns that subject so beloved of philosophers of religion: free-will and determinism. According to historical materialism, although there is freedom within the superstructure of society – the sphere of politics, law, philosophy, theology, the sphere of ideology – there is no place for human freedom in the base. The sphere of the base is the sphere of the laws of nature which operate 'with iron necessity', and which Marx assures us leave no room for individual responsibility. This historical materialist determinism has of course been of considerable embarrassment to Marxist philosophers.

The problem, however, lies not with Marx but with his followers. The freedom which they are so keen to preserve is in fact a bourgeois concept, literally. The bourgeois revolution in all of its ramifications depends on the assertion of individual liberty: *laissez faire, laissez aller, laissez passer*. But this freedom, hailed by the bourgeoisie as a moral virtue, was experienced by the working class as a vice. That same freedom to act out of self-interest was the source of oppression suffered by those who could not exercise it themselves. Those ravioli revolutionaries, those staff club socialists who are in good standing with their bourgeois colleagues, seek to explain away Marx's complete disinterest in such liberty. In doing so they not only misrepresent what Marx states so clearly, but they also do a grave disservice to the cause to which Marx dedicated his life.

As befits a messianic philosopher, Marx – this John the Baptist of the new moral age, this Moses who saw the promised land but was never privileged to enter into it – came with words of judgment as well as promise. He had words which were calculated to instil fear into the rulers of this world, as well as words of hope for the oppressed. And were the oppressed and heavy-laden worried about the loss of freedom in the sphere of the base? Not a bit of it, because they understood the positive implications of historical materialism. Bourgeois freedom was not their right but their enemy. And since in the historical sequence of social revolutions the bourgeoisie had now come to power, economic oppression would be the order of things for generations to come, for the foreseeable future. But now in the midst of their suffering they heard a prophetic voice ring out to condemn and to promise. Did Marx tell them that one day they could become bourgeois? Did he tell them that in the course of time the bourgeoisie would become more considerate? No, the source of hope for the future lay not with the bourgeoisie at all, but with a higher power, with a force which would bring such oppression to an end with or without the co-operation of the oppressors. Historical materialism was proclaimed like the messianic message of old: God's will will be done and the gates of hell shall not prevail against it. The new age and with it the end of oppression will come about inexorably, and with the impartiality of natural law. This is freedom. Those with ears to hear can join in and support that movement in history: others can ignore it at their peril and be crushed by it. That is the messianic message of historical materialism: it is good news to the poor. It is not science: it is faith. It is not materialism but morality. If freedom is the first issue arising from historical materialism, we now turn to the second, faith.

In the light of what has just been said, it should not surprise us that Marxism has about it the air of a messianic rather than a scientific movement. In 1847 the First Congress of the Communist League was held in London. Marx was unable to attend, but Engels prepared a document for it. The *Draft of a Communist Confession of Faith* is set out in the catechetical style of questions and answers. The Answer to Question 14, for example, sets out the fundamental proposition concerning historical materialism which we have just discussed. It is faith, not fact.

> We are also aware that revolutions are not made deliberately and arbitrarily, but that everywhere and at all times they are the necessary consequence of circumstances which are not in any way whatever dependent either on the will or on the leadership of individual parties or of whole classes.

This is the faith of Marx and Engels, that history is moving inexorably towards a moral goal and that this outcome is not subject to the whims or passions of men.

I have described this as a position of faith and not fact. The facts of history as we observe and experience them might well seem on balance to discredit historical materialism. But then faith can be sustained for long periods in face of facts to the contrary. I wish to illustrate this from the apostle Paul, and then from Marx himself.

Through Paul's letters we glimpse a life of hardship, disappointment and constant setbacks. Objectively speaking, events counted against the message which Paul preached. But faith experiences such things differently. 'And we know that all things work together for good to them that love God . . .' (Rom. 8.28). Despite everything, faith does not lose hope: it perceives in adversity the signs of victory. But this is also the position of Marx. For example in 1863, writing about the American Civil War, Marx reflected on the victory of the Confederate army in Maryland, and the defeat not only of the Union army, but of Lincoln, whom Marx greatly admired, and of the moral cause at the root of the conflict. Objectively the long-term outcome of the struggle looked to be going in the favour of the 'pro-slavery rebellion'. But that is not Marx's reaction. 'Reason nevertheless prevails in world history.' This is not science, history or politics. It is the voice of faith, strongly reminiscent of the sentiments of Paul. In 1854 Marx had already expressed this faith in an article for the New York *Daily Tribune* on 'The English Middle Class': 'though temporary defeat may await the working class, great social and economical laws are in operation which must eventually insure their triumph.' Two years later, in a public lecture in London, he could express this ideological faith in Hegelian terms. 'On our part, we do not mistake the shape of the shrewd Spirit that continually manifests himself in all these contradictions.' Where did Marx get this faith from, that history is being directed by an unseen spiritual force which is independent of human will or intention? He got it of course from the master, who was quite capable of expressing his philosophy of history in theological terms. Hegel tells us that 'God lets men do as they please with their particular passions and interests; but the result is the accomplishment of – not their plans but his . . .' Marx's ideological faith derives from Hegel's philosophical faith, which is entirely dependent on the biblical doctrine of providence. The question is not whether Marx had a messianic faith, a faith that history is proceeding inexorably towards a moral goal, the establishment of what I have called the kingdom of righteousness. The question is whether such a messianic faith plays any real part in the life of Christians today.

In this article I have examined the messianic elements in the philosophical faith of Karl Marx. At the outset some might have thought that this would lead to the view that Marx's philosophy is but a distorted and truncated version of the true and final faith found within the church. If only that were the case! Instead we have seen again and again that the central features of Marx's messianic faith point to embarrassing gaps in Christian messianic faith. Is this world being redeemed, or is redemption a metaphysical transaction which leaves this world unchanged – and unchecked? Is history moving towards a moral goal, to the achievement of justice and peace on earth, or is no one at the controls? Has it no inner fabric after all. And if there is no assurance that Christ is the reason of all things, the inner logic guiding us towards the kingdom of righteousness, what is the basis of the proclamation of good news to the poor?

Notes

1. Quotations from Marx are taken from two standard editions:
(a) Karl Marx/Friedrich Engels, *Werke*, Berlin 1964
(b) Karl Marx/Friedrich Engels, *Collected Works*, London. Page references to these and other works quoted are to be found in Alistair Kee, *Marx and the Failure of Liberation Theology*, London 1990.

Messiahs and Messianisms: Reflections from El Salvador

Jon Sobrino

The First World does not seem to go in for Messiahs or messianisms. It has no room for utopias of the poor and shows a distinct 'deficit' of leaders willing to head them. And as the First World decides what is real in this world, and as it has decided – from a modernist, post-modernist or merely pragmatic standpoint – that both Messiahs and messianisms are unreal and suspect, it follows that speaking about them is out of fashion. Add to this the fact that history – and this is something that must be taken seriously – has shown the dangers both phenomena can bring with them: populisms, paternalisms, dictatorships, simple-mindedness, fatality, aggressivity, and the conclusion has to be that there is little to be said about them. At best they will be tolerated, with benevolent superiority, as a fault of developing nations. . . .

Nevertheless, whatever name one gives them, the poor of this world, who make up the great majority of its population, need utopias, which can be as simple as conditions that make life possible, but which are no less real for that, since life is precisely what the poor cannot take for granted, and for which *there is still no room* in this world. And this same Third World of the poor continues to hope for the emergence of leaders with hearts of flesh, not stone, to give them hope and offer them ways to live.

Furthermore, here in El Salvador – as in other countries of Latin America – the poor found their voice some years ago and set about producing their hopes in the form of popular movements, hopes that found an echo in pastors such as Archbishop Romero and in intellectuals such as Ignacio Ellacuría. It is true that, empirically, such movements have not had startling successes – partly through their own errors and more basically because they have not been tolerated by the First World – but it is also true that they have achieved important results,[1] and that they have once again posited, not in pure conceptual terms, but in reality, the need for and meaning of Messiahs and messianisms. Remember that Ignacio Ellacuría's last work – his real theological testament – was on the subject of utopia and prophecy.[2]

For this basic reason – the need the crucified peoples have of utopias, messianic expectations or whatever one cares to call them – I am, without being an expert in exegesis or church history, writing about them, since 'Messianism has always been and will be the best antidote to the problems of the present, opening out on a future laden with hope'[3] – in words that are those of an expert.

1. The Third World's fear: a Christ without a kingdom

The loss of messianism not only has socio-political roots but in some measure begins straight after Christ's resurrection. So the question is both ecclesial and theological; it consists in the fact that the name of the *mediator* (the risen Christ) has come to relegate the *mediation* (bringing about the will of God, what Jesus called the kingdom of God, messianic hopes) to second place. Two things, in my view, have happened: the mediator has been given priority over his mediation, and the mediator has effectively come to be understood more on the *Son of God* model than on that of *Messiah*.

(a) A paradox: the 'de-messianization' of Christ

After the resurrection, *Christ*, which means *Messiah*, became the proper name of Jesus of Nazareth. It appears pragmatically as such in the kerygma, 'God has made this Jesus whom you crucified both Lord and Christ' (Acts 2.36), and is maintained in all strata of the New Testament. And this name became something so defining that it was also used to designate those who believed in Jesus, so that 'the disciples were . . . called Christians' (Acts 11.26, for the first time, at Antioch). This fact is obvious, but it is also obvious that the title of Messiah, applied to the risen Christ as something central, came to lose actuality and specificity. There were no doubt good reasons for this, but the final outcome is the paradox which one can, provocatively, call the de-messianization of Christ, that is: the de-messianization of the Messiah.

This process of de-messianization was made possible through the very ambiguity of the concept of *Messiah*. On the one hand it is clear that by calling him *Messiah* the first Christians were affirming that in the risen Christ a historical hope of Israel was being fulfilled: the appearance of a saviour; on the other hand, it is not very clear what model of saviour – among the many put forward in the Old Testament – Jesus could be said to conform to, since in the course of the Old Testament the Messiah had been thought of variously as king, then, after the failure of the monarchy, as high priest, as prophet and even as suffering servant. This king, moreover, could be either a warrior king, or a just and peaceful king. Victory over enemies could be achieved either through the direct action of God, or through the miracles worked by the Messiah. And as time went on and history gave the lie to the immediate fulfilment of this hope, the Messiah became an eschatological figure, that is, the object of ultimate hope for the future. We also know that Jesus never stated clearly whether he saw himself as the Messiah or not – remember the 'messianic secret' –, still less what sort of Messiah.

Without going into exegetical analysis of the question, what does seem clear is that after his resurrection, Jesus was understood as *saviour* and so could be called messiah, but the *salvation* he brings no longer seems to include a central element of messianism: that salvation is the historical salvation of an oppressed people, both outwardly and inwardly. Christ is not presented as the Messiah who, particularly since the Exile, is associated with the hope of the poor, as the just king who will finally impart justice, defend the weak and bring about reconciliation and solidarity.

(i) The hope of salvation in *history* is being replaced by transcendent salvation. This does not mean that the New Testament no longer gives any importance to earthly realities – its moral demands, with their call to charity, care for the weak and the like, prove that it does – but all these are now seen more as ethical requirements than as the central fact of Jesus by virtue of his messiahship. Salvation is concentrated, furthermore, on forgiveness of sins and turned into salvation in the *singular*. There is no more mention of the salvations in the *plural*, of body and soul, mentioned in the Gospels, but a concentration on inner salvation.

(ii) The correlative of messianic hopes is no longer the *people* with their collective hopes, but the individual. Again, this does not mean that the idea of 'collectivity' has disappeared from the New Testament, since what develops out of faith in Christ is precisely a community, and the nascent *ekklesia* expresses its own identity in terms that all imply collectivity: people, body, temple. . . . But on the other hand it is also true that concrete hopes of the peoples as such do disappear – what we would today call their social and political hopes (just as basically human as individual hopes): that slavery should cease and freedom reign, that wars should cease and peace reign, that repression should cease and justice reign; above all, that death should cease and life reign. . . . What is happening is that the 'messianic' hopes which the Messiah should fulfil are disappearing.

(iii) More specifically, there is a lessening importance given in understanding of the Messiah to what in the prophetic tradition of the Old Testament is the direct correlative of messianic hopes: the *poor* within the people. It is they who hope for the 'just king' of Isaiah, for the Messiah who will bring justice to the orphans and widows and who will, therefore, be partial, on their side.

All this needs to be understood properly. I am not of course denying or undervaluing the positive message of the New Testament: that Jesus brings forgiveness of sins and salvation, but I do stress the major shift it brings about in understanding of the term *Messiah*, and especially through applying this to Jesus as a proper name. A simple way of testing whether this 'de-messianization' is factual or not would be to ask ourselves whether when we talk of Christ (*the Messiah*) today, it occurs to any of us to relate the risen Christ to the hopes of the poor of this world.

(b) Concentrating on the mediator at the expense of mediation

This brings us to a central problem in the New Testament, one which goes beyond the known step from Jesus to Christ, that is, from the Jesus who preached to the Christ who is preached. We are dealing with a change in the understanding of God's plan: the kernel of the kerygma is no longer directly the coming of the kingdom of God proclaimed by Jesus, but the appearance of Christ. Although mediator and mediated are still related, the 'good news' of God is now centred on Christ and not on the kingdom of God, more on the mediator (the one sent by God) than on the mediation (the reality of a world conformed to the will of God). In this way realities that were important for Jesus of Nazareth become expressed in a way that, while still showing a continuity between pre- and post-Easter, also show discontinuity. So the first believers went on hoping for salvation and relating this to Christ, now exclusively so, but this salvation is no longer expressed as 'kingdom of God', liberation from multiple, earthly and transcendent wants, but as more transcendent salvation (in the *parousia*), more personal (of the individual) and more religious (forgiveness of sins).

The historical reasons for this are varied: the expectation of an imminent parousia and the end of history, the happy de-nationalizing of understanding of the people of God, the small size of the early communities . . . All these made it improbable that the problems and hopes of the poor would be seen on a mass scale – structurally, we should say today – so as to respond to them in history. But, as I have said, the result is nevertheless paradoxical: the Messiah ceases to respond to the hopes of the people, or, in more technical terms, the mediation of God is pushed into the background while everything seems to be concentrated on the appearance of the mediator.[4]

Furthermore, the mediator becomes understood more in his relation to the person of God (which was to be expressed in the titles of Lord and Son) than in his relation to the kingdom of God, as implied in the title Messiah. To put it in current terms, Jesus comes to appear as sacrament of the Father, the historical presence of God in the world, and this – good news, no doubt – is the most that can happen in history. In this way, although the name Christ (Messiah) is applied to Jesus as a proper name – with all this implies for the salvation of the poor, for the kingdom of God – the most distinctive element becomes the emphasis on Jesus' relationship with God, with the person of the Father, so that the prime understanding of him becomes as *Son of God* – even if this is not used as a proper name.[5] Again in other words, one can come to proclaim Jesus as the *auto-basileia tou Theou*, the kingdom of God in person – a fine statement, but also a dangerous one, since it can become a way of ignoring the *mediation* of God now that the *mediator* has appeared.

What is being expressed here in abstract form has had serious consequences for the history of faith and of theology, which have, sometimes implicitly and sometimes explicitly, presupposed that just this issue of messianism shows a virtually absolute break between the Old and New Testaments, that this break is positive and essential to the new faith. Certainly there is something new after Easter, but we need to analyse carefully what it consists of and what its consequences are. Of course the New Testament rejects the concept of Messiah as political and warrior king, but it would be tragic to convert Christ into the Messiah of a purely spiritual kingdom without incarnation, into a universal Messiah without preference for the poor, without mercy towards their sufferings, without demands for justice from their oppressors.

Put another way, the danger consists in ignoring – at least by comparison with the Old Testament – the fact that the good news also applies to the mediation: that the world, God's creation, is to be made according to God's heart. The appearance of the mediator and his reality as sacrament of 'the person' of the Father pushes into the background the importance for God of 'his will' being put into effect over this world, of transforming the reality of this world.

If I may be allowed a little irony without being misunderstood, one sometimes has the impression that some Christians see the heavenly Father as now perfectly happy because the mediator, the Son, has appeared on this earth, even though his creation is still in a lamentable state. We know that by sending the Son, God himself is forever committed to his creation. In the oft-quoted words of Karl Rahner, in Jesus God has once and for all broken the symmetry of being possibly saviour and possibly condemning judge: now God *is* essentially saviour. But it is also appropriate to recall the words of Genesis, without rejecting them too quickly as anthropomorphic, and to apply them to what God might feel – today too – on seeing his creation: 'Yahweh saw that the wickedness of man was great on the earth . . . Yahweh regretted having made man on the earth, and his heart grieved' (Gen. 6.5–6). This indignation on the part of God is what we need to recover and maintain if we are to revalue the importance God attaches to his mediation too, *God's* creation.

2. The Third World's need: a Messiah with a kingdom for the poor

Some readers – especially in the First World – might object to the above reflections on the grounds that this is how things were and one has to accept them as such. But the Third World – where, even the United Nations admit, things are getting worse – is still clamouring for mediation, as the New Testament also does in its way by sending us back to the Jesus of the Gospels. So let us consider a Messiah with a kingdom for the poor.

(a) The 're-messianization' of Christ

I have stressed that we must not ignore or play down the state of God's creation, and that we should not do it on the grounds that a definitive mediator has appeared. And one way of re-taking the situation of creation seriously – a christological way – is to 're-messianize' Christ, meaning to place him in relation to the hopes of the poor, to 'politicize' him, if you like. In order to do this, however, we need to avoid two prejudices, which are never wholly overcome and constantly return in history, as shown in the Latin American church after the audacity of Medellin and the serene affirmation of Puebla.

The first is that, although Jesus certainly did not seek to be a political Messiah, let alone king, and did not use political power, this does not mean that he did not seek to shape the *polis*, nor use a certain power to do so, even though this power was not political or military, but the power of truth (proclamation of the utopia of the kingdom, denunciation and exposure of the anti-kingdom), the power of love (with its concrete expressions in mercy and justice) and the power of witness (his faithfulness even to the cross). What is wrong with denying the political aspect of the Messiah Jesus consists, then, not in denying his rejection of becoming a nationalistic warrior king and his spurning of a theocratic kingdom, but in stripping the concept of Messiah of the oppressions and hopes of human beings in society, on the one hand, and of the need to use some power, on the other, a power that does not cease to be *powerful* through being that of truth and love. Because it is powerful it is also conflictive, as the recent history of Latin America shows. What is wrong, then, is to deny or undervalue the saving relationship between Messiah and people.

The second prejudice to be exposed is reducing the question of the relationship between Jesus and politics to analysis of the title 'Messiah'. Methodologically, it should now be clear that one should not read the noun from the adjective, but the other way round. So we should not say 'Jesus is the Messiah', but 'Messiah? That's Jesus'. Now, if we approach the Gospels from this angle, we find that Jesus did regard the messianic hopes of the people, and the poor in particular, as something central; he does, that is, resemble the 'just and partial king' of Isaiah who seeks to instil right and justice, he does work mercy for the weak and does denounce oppressors.

What title is given to the Jesus shown in the Gospels is to some extent of secondary importance. What matters is that this Jesus expresses the central concerns of the messianic hopes of the poor in the Old Testament, while profoundly changing its theocratic, nationalistic, exclusive and military connotations. What the Synoptics do – of vital importance within the New Testament, as has been said often enough – is take us back to Jesus and to his essential relationship to the kingdom of God.[6] It is not so important for an understanding of Jesus' messianism whether the Synoptics give him the title of Messiah and in what form. The most important and decisive element is their presentation of Jesus in relation to the kingdom, since 'messianic hope was directed in the first place not torwards a specific and particular figure as toward the coming of the kingdom of God'.[7]

Today it is equally urgent to reclaim the title of Messiah, as much – formally – to avoid falling into the anomalous situation where 'Messiah' (Christ) is the commonest term used to refer to Jesus without it saying anything concrete, as – materially – not to deprive the poor of the world of hope. The first can and should be done in various ways. So José-Ignacio González Faus, for example, subtly reinterprets the meaning of the title in accordance with its potential for telling us what our hopes and attitudes should be today: crucial is his admonition that we are dealing with a 'crucified' Messiah, which militates against the temptation to wait for the 'magician' and delegate salvation to him, and it is vital to stress that Christian hope and praxis have to look to the kingdom.[8]

With regard to the second, the question has been brought out into the open again by liberation theology and resolved on principle by according Jesus the title of 'liberator'. The faith of Latin American Christians and the christology of liberation have given the title 'Messiah' back its deep significance and urgency.[9] This 'liberator' today sums up what is central to the primary meaning of the Messiah: someone will appear in history to bring salvation to the poor and oppressed; a just king will appear to free the mass of the people from their slaveries. This is how Jesus is seen by many in the Third World today. This does not imply a pure and simple return to the New Testament, still less seeing the liberator as a nationalistic, theocratic, warrior king. But it does mean recovering the essential: the one sent by God will have his eyes fixed on the poor of this world, with their slaveries and their hopes.

The historical situation of Latin America makes this recovery of the messianism of Jesus possible; it also makes it imperative. With or without the title of 'liberator', Jesus clearly has to be seen in this way, since any other would fail to do justice both to the reality of Latin America and to the reality of a Christ who is Jesus of Nazareth. And this, indeed, is what Puebla sanctioned by recognizing in 'many segments of the People of God . . . their search for the ever new face of Christ, who is the legitimate answer to their yearning for integral liberation' (173). This does not imply reducing the totality of Christ to what is expressed by the title 'liberator', or, more precisely, to a reductionist interpretation, against which Puebla warns: a Christ who is 'a politician, a leader, a revolutionary, or a simple prophet' (178). But it does both make possible and demand a christology that – beginning from the liberating messianism of Jesus – can unfold in totality.

(b) Messiah and Son

It seems clear to me that the title 'liberator' is essential for faith in Christ today, and this, too, is the way to 're-messianize' him. We must avoid the pitfalls: making 'the liberator' into a magical formula for solving all problems, or reducing Christ to responding to social problems only, ignoring other dimensions of human beings, including the poor, or fanaticizing and deceiving the poor in the name of an imminent liberation *quasi ex opere operata*. But the basic intuition holds good: Christ, by definition, is 'Messiah', and this messiahship can and – very largely – must be described as liberation. In the final analysis, it is somewhat paradoxical – and sad – to have to point out that Christ is 'liberator', but perhaps through the tautology 'Christ-liberator' we can recover for our times what it really means to be Christ.

It is not good for the mediation to disappear behind the mediator, as I have repeated here. But then, neither is the contrary good: for the mediator to disappear behind the mediation. And not just this: we need to point out that the mediator is not just Messiah but Son also, that Jesus has a basic relationship not only with the kingdom of God, but also with the Father. I state this not just to uphold what the New Testament and Christian tradition and orthodoxy say, but because experience shows that a Messiah who is Son is a more effective Messiah. To finish, I should like to illustrate this with two figures from El Salvador.

Archbishop Romero aroused, inspired, guided and upheld the messianic expectations of the Salvadorean people as no one else. There is no doubting this, and the people themselves proved it when, on 1 February 1992, as the first day of peace broke, they filled the 'martyrs' square' and to express their joy hung a huge placard on the façade of the cathedral: on it was a photo of Archbishop Romero with the words, 'Monsignor, you have risen again in your people.' What I want to add is that Mgr Romero was not only a good 'Messiah' but a *good* Messiah. He not only brought good news to the people, but was good news in himself, in how he acted.

And Mgr Romero was not only good, but holy,[10] intimately united to God, in such a way that people understood that he was not just a man of the people – which he was – but also a man of God, and that this did not distance him from ordinary men and women but brought him closer to them. In other words, Mgr Romero's personal holiness, his personal union with God,[11] in no way diminished his 'messianic' qualities, but increased them. Mgr Romero was an outstanding illustration of the historical efficacy of holiness.

By this I am trying to show that the thing mediated (the kingdom of God) is good news and the mediator (Jesus) is good news, that messianism and sonship are not mutually exclusive but complementary and that, therefore, Jesus can and should be proclaimed Messiah and Son, without one title taking anything away from the other. This is what Mgr Romero showed in our historical time, and he – what is more – ended like Jesus on the cross, uniting for ever Messiah, Son and Servant.

Given our faith and our situation in the Third World, what we need to do is to bring all this together. The poor are in urgent need of mediation: a kingdom of God that can bring their messianic hopes to fulfilment. They hope for a Messiah, the mediator, who will bring them this kingdom. And they want a holy mediator who – with the kingdom – can make the good God present to them. In the First World, hopes, and above all despairs, can be different, and therefore, perhaps, talk of messianism is a thing of the past. But in the Third World it is still a necessity.

Ignacio Ellacuría used to point these things out. I remember hearing him say – and this way surprise those who did not know him well – that 'the ultimate weapon of the church of the poor is holiness'. He believed and hoped, then, in a holy mediator. And, at the same time, to the end, stressed the need for the mediation. 'Only in a utopian way and in hope can one believe and dare, with all the poor and oppressed of the world, to turn back the course of history, subvert it and launch it in a different direction.'

Translated by Paul Burns

Notes

1. Here in El Salvador, the popular movements, political and religious, have developed important personal and social values: the priority of the community over the individual, of creativity over imposed receptivity, of celebration over commercialized amusement, of hope over conformity, of transcendence over blunt positivism. It is true that these movements have made mistakes and that neo-liberalism will have nothing to do with them, so that their future is uncertain. This is unfortunate, since their disappearance would mean a great social impoverishment for all.

2. 'Utopía y profetismo desde América Latina', in *Revista Latinoamericana de Teología* 17, 1989, 141–84. It is important to note that, among other things, Ellacuría establishes a dialectical relationship between utopia and prophecy: prophecy denounces what has to be eradicated, and this – though it may seem a minimum – is already a maximum. As Mgr Romero said: 'We have to defend the minimum which is God's maximum gift: life.'

3. A. Salas, *El mesianismo: promesas y esperanzas*, Madrid 1990, 77.

4. The reason for this concentration is already implicit in the resurrection. 'The resurrection and raising up of Jesus is, in effect, *bring together and concentrate* the eschatological action of God *in a single person*. The ineffable mystery of God who contains all without being contained is presented to us visibly and perceptibly only in the form of a man: the man Jesus' (H. Kessler, *La resurrección de Jesús*, Salamanca 1976, 199).

5. Walter Kasper puts it well: 'The profession of the divine sonship of Jesus is from then on the distinctive mark of being Christian', *Jesús el Cristo*, Salamanca 1986, 199 (ET *Jesus the Christ*, London and New York 1976).

6. This is the basic reason why Latin American christology goes back to the historical Jesus: not so much – as may happen in other places – to know what happened, but to reinstate the centrality of the kingdom of God. Cf. J. Sobrino, *Jesucristo liberador*, Madrid 1991, 143–77 (ET in preparation, Maryknoll NY and Tunbridge Wells 1993).

7. J. Imbach, *¿De quién es Jesús?*, Barcelona 1991, 96.

8. José-Ignacio González Faus, *La humanidad nueva. Ensayo de cristología*, Santander 1984, 256ff.

9. From this aspect, the most important thing about L. Boff's first book of christology was its title, *Jesucristo libertador*, Petrópolis 1971 (Jesus Christ Liberator).

10. In my article 'Political Holiness: A Profile', in *Concilium* 163, 18–23, I refer to Mgr Romero as an example of such holiness.

11. How important God was in his life was evident from his homilies. This sentence is from that of 10 February 1980, a month before his death: 'Who could grant me, beloved brothers and sisters, that the fruit of this preaching might be for each one of us to go and meet God!'

Christology and Jewish-Christian Relations

Rosemary Radford Ruether

The Christian affirmation that Jesus is the Christ arose out of a heritage of ideas in the Jewish tradition of the first century about the coming of a redemptive figure at the end-time of history. But this idea was so revised by Christian experience and theological reflection that it became largely incomprehensible and radically unacceptable to Judaism.

Christianity responded to this Jewish rejection of its claims by constructing an anti-Judaic 'left-hand' of christology which it used both to vilify Jews and also to repress and attack them in Christian societies. Such villification, repression and violence made christology all the more unacceptable to Jews. Is it possible in the last decade of the twentieth century, after two thousand years of this conflict, for Jews and Christians to enter into positive dialogue on this question of the Messiah?

In this article I will briefly summarize this construction of an anti-Judaic 'left-hand' of christology by Christianity, and its consequences for Jewish existence, particularly once Christian social life became organized as a Christian state or empire. I will then ask whether this anti-Judaic 'left-hand' can be removed from christology so that the affirmation that Jesus is the Christ for Christians ceases to demean Jews, religiously or socially. Finally, I will raise the question of how the Jewish and Christian hopes for a Messiah relate to the advent of messianic states or political entities which are claimed to be expressions of God's reign on earth.

Whether Jesus himself claimed to be the Messiah has been questioned by modern New Testament scholars. Some would see him, not as making this claim for himself, but rather as situating his mission and message in relation to a coming Son of Man and Reign of God.[1] Nevertheless there is no doubt that the Christian community after his death claimed messianic status for him, using several Jewish traditions about this figure (Davidic Messiah, Son of Man).

Yet the stark reality that Jesus' mission and message had ended on the cross of Roman judicial execution was a profound crisis for early Christianity. Any claim that Jesus was the Messiah had to be constructed to explain this scandal. Christianity did so by uniting several ideas from the Jewish tradition that had not been so joined before. It fused the messianic idea with the Suffering Servant of Isaiah 53 to affirm that the suffering and death of the Son of Man are necessary for redemption.

Early Christians separated redemption as an inward relation to God from the transformation of historical evils in the Kingdom of God, which was postponed to a future Second Coming of Christ in glory. Christians also connected the Messiah as the redemptive figure of the end-time with cosmological concepts, such as the Wisdom of God and the Logos of God, so that this redemption won by Christ was seen as restoring and renewing the original and true nature of creation.

These developments made the Christian claims about Jesus as the Christ incompatible with the Jewish understanding of the Messiah. For Judaism the coming of the Messiah cannot be separated from the coming of the Kingdom of God, the transformation of the evils of history.[2] The Christian claim that this event had already happened, even though there was no evidence that the evils of history were being overcome, or that Christians were contributing to such amelioration, made no sense in the context of the Jewish understanding of the Messiah. For Judaism, messianic claims are to be tested by the reality of their ethical and socio-political fruits.

When Christians sought to preach their christological interpretation of the Hebrew scriptures in the synagogues of Palestine or the Diaspora, the rabbinic leaders mobilized themselves to exclude them. Christians responded by incorporating into their understanding of the necessity of the suffering of the Son of Man the idea that (the leadership class of) his own people must reject him. Vilification of the leadership classes of temple and synagogue Judaism as 'hypocrites and blind guides' became a part of the Christian proclamation.[3]

This growing estrangement was taking place at a time when Palestinian Jewry was drawn into two periods of revolt against the Roman empire (66–73 and 132–36 CE). These revolts were fed by messianic fervour through apocalyptic literature. After the fall of the temple in 70 CE the surviving rabbinic leadership consolidated itself as the normative guardians of Jewish religious and communal survival. It excluded messianic activism and strictly banned sectarian groups, such as Christians.

Christian polemic against Jewish leaders as blind guides came to include the idea that their rejection of Jesus as the Christ discredits their authority and changes the relation of the Jewish people as a whole to God. These views shaped the writings that became the New Testament. These anti-Judaic themes were further developed in the *Adversus Judaeos* writings of the Church Fathers during the second to fourth centuries.

The *Adversus Judaeos* writings centre on two themes: the rejection of the Jews by God and the election of the Gentiles, and the abrogation and spiritual fulfilment of the Law and the temple cult. God's rejection of the Jews is a divine response to the Jewish rejection of Jesus as the Christ, but this rejection itself is seen as the culmination of a long history of Jewish apostasy. The Jews are said to have always rejected the prophets and even to have killed them. Beginning with the Golden Calf they continually turned from God and worshipped idols.

In writers of the late fourth century, such as John Chrysostom, this negative picture of the Jews takes on demonic proportions. The Jews are painted as preternatural embodiments of evil with superhuman appetites for every depravity of flesh and spirit.[4] The main texts for this extreme picture of Jewish perversity were the Hebrew prophets themselves. However, the prophetic writings use descriptions of fallenness to call the Jewish people to repentance, whereas the church fathers split the negative language of judgment from the positive call to repentance and future hope. The negative side is read as descriptive of the historical reality of the Jews, while the positive side is claimed as the future promise of Christ and the church.

The culminating crime of this evil history is then read to be the rejection and killing of the Messiah. It is Chrysostom that uses the term 'deicide' for this event.[5] In his view it is a crime of treason and *lèse majesté* against the Sovereign of the Universe. For criminals of such a stamp no vituperation is too extreme, and he continually speaks of Jews as devils, their synagogues as brothels of the Devil. For this final crime the patience of God with the Jews has been exhausted. Their election and favour with God has been revoked, and they are driven into exile. Their city has been destroyed and their cult place ravished. They are to be in captivity under their enemies, there never to know any cessation of misery until the end of time.

By contrast, according to the patristic writers, the former enemies of God, the Gentiles, have now been converted and become God's new elect

people. Scriptural texts about the ingathering of nations are read as
predictions of this coming Gentile church, but excluding the apostate
Jews.[6] After the Constantinian establishment this ingathering of the
nations is identified with the world church joined to the Roman empire.
Bishop Eusebius, the eulogist of Constantine, identifies Christendom with
the millennial reign of Christ on earth.[7]

The church fathers stress the idea of a substitution of the faithful Gentile
church for the unfaithful Jews, rather than the Pauline view of the
ingrafting of the church into Israel. Nevertheless, they assume an ongoing
relation of God to the Jews, although now in a negative form of wrath and
reprobation. The Jews, although exiles and wanderers within the Christian era, are eventually to be converted. In Augustine's *City of God*, this
eschatological conversion of the Jews is reserved for the end-times. Prior to
the return of Christ Elijah would be sent to earth to convert the Jews and
thus to gather them into the community of final salvation.[8]

These anti-Judaic interpretations of scripture would have had little
effect on the status of the Jews had it not been for the fateful incorporation
of the Christian church into the Roman empire by Constantine as his
official religion. This gaining of political power allowed Christian anti-
Judaic views to be translated into both Christian Roman law and also canon
laws that could be enforced for the whole society.

Civil and canonical legislation in the fourth to sixth centuries marginalized the Jews in Christian society. They were removed from access to civil
offices, forbidden to hold Christian slaves (Christians were not so
forbidden and large-scale manufacturing and agriculture depended on
slave labour), and special taxes were imposed on them.[9] Yet although
marginalized, Jews were not excluded as a social and religious group. This
is notable because by 380 CE all other non-orthodox groups (pagans,
Christian heretics) were proscribed in the Christian empire.

In this period incidents of popular riots also broke out in which
synagogues were burned by Christian mobs. The Christian emperors in
some cases called for these mobs to pay restitution to the Jewish
community. This role of protection of the Jews would be taken over by
Popes and Christian princes in the Latin Middle Ages. In Christian
treatment of the Jews a complex pattern developed, consisting of official
disabilities and popular violence, but also a limited right to exist within
Christian societies, in which Christian authorities acted as guarantors of
this minimal 'protection'.[10]

This policy of 'protection of the Jews' flowed from the side of Christian
belief that saw the Jews as eventually to be converted to Christ. In some

sense Christian salvation was incomplete until the Jews had been reconciled to Christ. Thus it became the responsibility of the church to enforce not only divine reprobation, but also protection of the Jews, for the purpose of this future reconciliation. Official Christian theory and policy towards Jews was repressive and often ambivalent; but it was not genocidal.

How then did modern antisemitism arise in the heart of Christian Europe in modern times and take the form of a systematic attempt at Jewish genocide? The discussion of the continuity and discontinuity between Christian anti-Judaism and Nazi antisemitism is too complex to go into in detail in this article. Suffice it to say that there was continuity in the heritage of hostility and social marginalization, but there was also a decisive discontinuity in the shift from religious to racial terms of reproach.

For the Christian tradition, the 'final solution to the Jewish question' was conversion. The Jews should not be eliminated from Christian Europe; they must be preserved for the final reconciliation. But when the reproach against the Jews became biological, then conversion as a 'solution' to 'what is wrong with the Jews' was ruled out. The solution became instead, for the Nazis, physical extermination. The church's guilt for the Holocaust resides, not only in having set the stage for the negative stereotypes of the Jews which were used by Nazism, but also for not having acted decisively, out of at least its own minimal tradition of protection, against genocide.

The horrors of the Nazi death camps are so profound that to speak of reconstructing christology in the light of the Holocaust seems almost trivial. Repentant silence seems more appropriate. There is no suggestion here that simply rethinking theological formulas *per se* is an adequate response to this terrible history. Healing must take place on many different levels. Nevertheless, re-examining those theological patterns which shaped, and continue to shape, the Christian view of the Jews as the negative side of their affirmation that Jesus is the Christ is one element in that repentance that is required.

Christian teaching, both on the academic level and also on the popular level of preaching, liturgy and catechetics, needs to reform all those patterns of thought in which binary opposites – 'Law/grace', 'Old era/New era', 'Old Covenant/New Covenant' – set the Jews and the Jewish religion as the 'type' of the negative and incomplete over against Christ and the Christian gospel as the good and the completed truth. Such dialectical tensions of external and internal, unfulfilment and fulfilment, exist within each community. They do not divide the one from the other.

In patristic Christianity the dialectical structure of prophetic faith was split apart so that the positive side of forgiveness and promise was predicated of the Christian church, while the negative side of divine wrath, judgment and rejection was read out against the Jews. This false exegesis fundamentally distorted the meaning of prophetic faith. The Hebrew scriptures, which contain the tradition of Jewish self-criticism and repentance, were turned into a remorseless projection of negative stereotypes. The church thereby divorced itself from the tradition of prophetic self-criticism and was made to appear triumphal and perfect.

Although practically no Christian scholar of the Hebrew Bible would read the prophets in this way today, this still requires some rethinking of the way Christians presume that the 'Old Testament' predicts and is fulfilled in the 'New Testament'. It also demands the untangling of the sectarian polemic that appears in the New Testament itself. Here Christian exegesis needs to move through two levels of critique.

First, we should understand that prophetic criticism is valid only as internal criticism, a criticism that springs from commitment to the redemptive future of those people whom one criticizes. It is fundamentally distorted when it is used from outside simply as the rejection of another poeple with whom one feels no common life. Whatever was true in New Testament denunciations of legalism or hypocrisy in the religion of Jesus' day must be seen as a criticism of Jesus' own religion, not the religion of some alien group, the Jews, with whom he did not identify himself.

This means that, as Christians now stand as a separate people from the Jewish people, such criticism can be validly applied only as self-questioning. We have to ask ourselves to what extent our own understanding of Christian faith has become external, 'clerical' and lacking in authentic spirituality and concern for those 'unclean ones' who become the victims of our righteousness.

But this internalization of criticism will not overcome the anti-Judaic stereotypes if it leaves the Christian with the impression that Christians might fall into legalistic error, but such error is generic to the nature of Judaism. We must change the language by which Christian self-criticism still takes the stereotyping of Judaism as its negative point of reference. Christian seminaries have to include in their studies an accurate understanding of the rabbinic tradition and Jesus' place in it.

A positive understanding of figures such as Hillel must correct the negative use of terms such as 'Pharisee'. Christians need to be prepared to interpret the New Testament language with the same kind of nuanced appreciation of the Jesus' Judaism that they would wish to convey about their own Christianity: namely a religion that contains both prophetic vision and also the dangers of institutional deformation.

Other binary terms that call for new thinking are particularism and universalism, and Old and New Covenant. Christians have seen themselves as manifesting the new universal 'people of God', drawn from all nations, that superseded the ethnic particularism of Judaism. It is true that Judaism remains tied to an ethnic understanding of Jewish peoplehood in a way that Christianity is not, although this Jewish 'ethnicity' itself has become multi-racial and multi-cultural in the course of Jewish dispersion. It is also true that such ethnicity can be deformed into ethnocentrism.

However, Christians err in failing to recognize that they, too, however ethnically plural, are also a particularity of religion and culture *vis-à-vis* other religious, cultural groups. Christian claims of universality lend themselves to cultural imperialism in which they assume that their religion is the only religion that validly relates them to God. All other religious identities are spurious, demonic and do not mediate relation to God. Only in so far as people incorporate themselves into this one true human identity do they achieve salvation. This is false universalism, or the absolutization of one particularism of religious culture.

One solution to anti-Judaism and Christian false universalism, proposed by Paul van Buren, is to return to the affirmation that God is the God of the Jews in a unique sense and has chosen the Jews to be his elect people in an irreplaceable manner. The only way Christianity can share in this relationship to God is to acknowledge that they are ingrafted into the Jewish covenant and are only the Gentile extension of that one covenant.[11]

While there is validity in recognizing the Jewish roots of the basic Christian concepts, such as covenant, I think that Van Buren's solution sells out the profound insight that God is indeed a God of all nations and not of one nation only. We should not construct a new exclusivism of covenant and election, applied to one people alone, in which the experiences of God of other peoples, including those of the church through Jesus, are made simply subservient appendages. I prefer to think in terms of plural covenantal relations to God in which many peoples can find their own particularity, but in mutual affirmation, rather than in competitive negation, of other people.

Only God is finally one and universal. Humanity, earth and the whole creation can be thought of as one because God is its source and goal of life. But there is no final perspective on humanity available through the historical identity of any one people, short of that messianic gathering up of all peoples that has not yet happened (and could only happen authentically by finding what is authentic in each, not the negation of all others for one privileged group). The relativization of the Christian perspective thus demands a significant modification of the assumption that Christianity already has the 'end-time' perspective.

All of these efforts to rethink the binary dualisms that have shaped Christian theology finally must centre upon christology. Since the anti-Judaic 'left hand of Christian thought' was and is tied to the way christological affirmation has been understood, it is not possible to purge these anti-Judaic patterns without rethinking the christological theses on which they are based.

The key to rethinking christology lies, in my view, in a theology of hope. That means reformulating the understanding of Jesus as the Christ as proleptic and contextual, rather than as fulfilled and final. The proleptic understanding of Jesus as the Christ is already quite familiar to modern theologians, ever since it became apparent in the late nineteenth century that ideas like Messiah and the Kingdom of God really did relate to a historical transformation of the world and not simply to an inward relation to God. This recognition forced theologians to reckon with the unfulfilled nature of those external historical transformations which the Jewish tradition identified with the coming of the Messiah and Christianity postponed to the 'Second Coming'.

To say that Jesus is the Christ proleptically allows us to make theological sense of the New Testament in its Jewish context. Reading the Jesus event as the fulfilment of messianic expectations two thousand years ago, with little evident improvement in human moral realities, either denies historical reality or makes it irrelevant. Hope for a transformed and redeemed history is still the core of messianic hope. But its fulfilment is still as much ahead of us as Christians, as it is ahead of the Jews.

The experience of Jesus' resurrection stands as the foretaste of that proleptic future in which evil is overcome. What is obvious as historical 'fact' is the cross; the realities of human animosity, betrayal, refusal to repent and will to kill the prophetic announcer still define our human historical reality. The resurrection means that, in spite of the historical victory of evil over good, God continues to affirm the truth of his prophet, Jesus. God has snatched him up on the 'right hand'. In his name this hope continues to be announced, and we are called to continue to walk his path of risky witness.

But the fulfilment, the redemption of the earth, the wiping away of every tear, the establishment of peace and justice and unity of all people with one another and with God, all this is still the unrealized future. Here and now we, as much as the Jewish people, struggle with an unresolved history, holding on to our experience of the risen Jesus as our basis for refusing to take evil as the last word and our continued faith that God will win in the end. Dialogue between Christians and Jews blossoms when those memories and hopes can be seen as analogous and mutual, rather than as mutually exclusive.[12]

Such dialogue also demands that Christians take a second step, recognizing not only the proleptic character, but also the paradigmatic and contextual nature of Jesus' messianic identity. Jesus, the prophetic announcer put to death, in whose name we are called to walk the path of risky witness, is our paradigmatic story. But this does not mean that it is the only story by which hope in the midst of adversity may be mediated. Jesus is not the only name that can be named in heaven and on earth; he is *our* name.

This need not exclude other people continuing their struggle for redemption through other names and other stories; namely, the Jews, for whom the name of Jesus did not become paradigmatic or revelatory, and who still found themselves on the Exodus and the Torah as their memory and their Way. The goal of dialogue is not to establish the Jesus paradigm as the paradigm Jews must accept, but to arrive at a mutual recognition of analogous paradigms that can remove the negative force of the cross of Jesus as the lynching post of the Jewish people.

The recognition by Christians that messianic hope implies real historical transformation of social relations raises anew the question of how we discern the signs of the times and differentiate between true and false messianic advents. How do we keep from, once again, clothing sinful human projects in the glorious mantle of the Kingdom of God and thus turning error into self-enclosed idolatry?

We have seen this mistake many times in Christian history and its secular heirs. The blasphemous character of the Eusebian eulogy of Constantine as the representative of Christ on earth, and his empire as the realized Kingdom of God, is all too obvious today. So too the absolutistic claims of Marxist revolutions to be realizing the 'classless society' are more than discredited. Even the much more tentative rhetoric of the victorious Sandinista revolution, savagely undermined by ten years of Contra warfare and the reestablishment of a dependent regime, is now so ground into the dust of defeat that one scarcely knows how to speak again of hope in that land.

Today this question also confronts the Jewish people as well. After two thousand years of statelessness, the founding of the state of Israel is, for many Jews and Christians, a fulfilment of prophecy and the first stage of a messianic stage. Over against the Holocaust, the state of Israel's messianic status seems to many to be an unquestionable 'right'. Those who question its goodness are decried as anti-semites who refuse to accept the right of the Jews to exist in security in a state of their own.

But can we ignore the price paid for this state: the confiscation of the homes and lands of two million Palestinians, the ongoing toll in violent repression of Palestinian rights to their own land and state; the preparations for nuclear war on the side of Israel, which evoke like preparations among the Arabs, the spectre of nuclear Holocaust in the Middle East? However one may weigh the relative faults on each side, what must be said is that we are not closer to messianic times in 1992, after forty-four years of Israel's existence in the Middle East.

The neo-orthodox 'eschatological reservation' may be the timely word to say against all such temptations to accord human efforts messianic status. But does this mean that there is no better or worse in human affairs, no significant distinction between brutal tyranny and those fragile flowers of justice and love which, though not perfect, at least give us some taste of the right path?

Messianic hopes are not simply about life after death or an inward reconciliation with God that makes no apparent impact on human affairs. It is about ameliorating the conditions of real human life on earth, moving towards a little more love and justice and peace. How do we discern when that is happening amid a welter of conflicting claims?

Perhaps our surest reality test to discern messianic 'signs of the times' is when the good things are genuinely mutual; when the salvation of one community does not spell the damnation of another; when the events that give us hope do not cast others into despair; when the realization of our 'promised land' is not purchased through the exile of others. When these moments of inclusive healing take place, then we have a right to say, 'Yes, we have tasted the Holy One in our midst'.

Notes

1. Rudolf Bultmann, *Theology of the New Testament*, Vol. 1, New York and London 1951, 26–32.

2. Gershom Scholem, *The Messianic Idea in Judaism*, New York 1971, 1–36.

3. Rosemary Ruether, *Faith and Fratricide: The Theological Roots of Anti-Semitism*, New York 1974, 70–94.

4. *John Chrysostom, Homilies against the Jews*, ET C. Mervyn Maxwell, Ph D

dissertation, University of Chicago, 1966; also Ruether, *Faith and Fratricide*, 173–181.

5. Chrysostom, Homily 1.7, col. 854 (Maxwell, 32).

6. Ruether, *Faith and Fratricide*, 137–144.

7. Eusebius, *Ecclesiastical History*, X.4.3; also his *Oration on Constantine, Nicene and Post-Nicene Fathers*, vol. 1, 2nd series, ed. Philip Schaff and Henry Wace, New York 1890, 561ff.

8. Augustine, *City of God*, XX.29.

9. James S. Seaver, *The Persecution of the Jews in the Roman Empire*, Kansas 1952; also Ruether, *Faith and Fratricide*, 186–92.

10. For example, on the policy of Pope Gregory I, see Ruether, *Faith and Fratricide*, 200.

11. Paul Van Buren, *Christian Theology of the People Israel*, New York 1983; for a critique of Van Buren's view, see Rosemary and Herman Ruether, *The Wrath of Jonah: The Crisis of Religious Nationalism in the Israeli-Palestinian Conflict*, San Francisco, CA 1989, 211–15.

12. Jacob Neusner has proposed this model of analogical stories as the basis for Jewish-Christian dialogue; see his 'There has Never Been a Judaeo-Christian Dialogue, But There Can Be One', in *Cross Currents*, Spring 1992, 3–25.

The Church as Communion

The document from the 'Congregation for the Doctrine of Faith' entitled 'Letter to the Bishops of the Catholic Church on Some Aspects of the Church Understood as Communion', dated 15 June 1992, is not an ecumenical text but an internal Roman Catholic instruction. Nor is it a theological text with arguments and evidence, but a decree making claims which are not to be discussed, but to be obeyed. Although the text is not an invitation but a demarcation, it should not be left unanswered. As a Protestant theologian, I shall first go into the statements about 'Ecclesial Communion and Ecumenism' in section V.17, 18 and then discuss the theses on unity and multiplicity in church communion.

In the text, expressions like 'non-Catholic Churches', 'Churches separated from the See of Peter' and 'Christian communities' alternate. In one paragraph of V.17 the Orthodox Churches are given the title 'particular churches', though in the next section they are demoted to being 'venerable Christian communities'. The Protestant churches are rated 'ecclesial communities' although it is claimed that 'they have not retained the apostolic succession and a valid Eucharist'. I find these varying descriptions with their different value judgments unworthy of ecumenical dialogue. In dialogue it is proper to use one's partners' own names, not to give them names of one's own devising. One can also think of names for Rome from the theological controversies of the confessional era which would not be appreciated there.

It is asserted that the nature of the 'venerable Christian communities' as 'particular churches' has been wounded (V.17), and that in the case of the 'ecclesial church communities' the 'wound is even deeper'; the separation even injures the Roman Catholic church, 'in that it hinders the complete fulfilment of her universality in history' (17). Is that really the only pain that is felt in Rome? Certainly the body of Christ has suffered harm as a result of the divisions of the church. The ecumenical movement came into being on the basis of this insight. But the excommunication of the Orthodox church in the eleventh century and of the Protestant churches in the sixteenth century was on the initiative of Rome, and the 'Congregation of Faith', which at that time was still called the 'Holy Inquisition', inflicted so many wounds on the body of Christ that self-knowledge and penitence would be more appropriate than putting the blame on others. We have not forgotten our martyrs. Fortunately the Orthodox, Protestant, Anglican and Old Catholic churches are preventing Rome from 'fulfilling her universality', for the Roman centralist system itself stands in the way of the universality of the gospel. And today as a Protestant theologian with catholic sensibilities I can only repeat with pain and grief what José Marti said at the time of the excommunication of Eduardo McGlynn, the priest of the poor. 'The church does not fight against its enemies but against its best sons' – and also against its best friends.

The non-Roman Catholic churches in the ecumenical world are quite ready for communion with Rome, but never for communion under Rome. For Christ's sake, there will be no ecumenism which consists in a return to Rome, such as the document wishes in V.18. There could be discussion only over a papacy reformed in the light of the gospel. The bishop of Rome is our venerable and important brother in Christ, but he is not the 'head of the church' (12). For the churches of Christ, Christ alone is the head, and is present through his Spirit in word, sacrament and community. Where Christ is, there is the church: *ubi Christus, ibi Ecclesia.*

The 'church in and of the churches', as Vatican II puts it, is formed by the *communion of the Holy Spirit*, which brings together the communion of human beings, the communion of creation (which is quite unknown to the document), and the communion of the triune God. The primacy of the bishop of Rome came about in history, as did also the historical form of a partial church. To see this as an 'element of the essence' of the true church is an unprovable assertion, which only serves to remove this form of the unity of the church from the discussion.

The church as a whole is not a 'product' of the individual churches, nor must it be described as the 'mother' of the particular churches (9). Causal thought is simplistic, and does not do justice to complex, living reality. Ecumenically we understand the unity of the churches as a relationship of reciprocal conditioning and interpenetration. The presence of Christ is experienced both in the churches and between them, wherever we are gathered in his name. Catholicity is a mark of the presence of Christ. It extends far beyond the Roman Catholic form of the Church.

The document from the 'Congregation of Faith' does not keep to what the

Contributors

WILLEM BEUKEN was born in the Netherlands in 1931. He became a Jesuit in 1949 and was ordained priest in 1961. After studying at the Biblical Institute in Rome he gained his doctorate at the University of Utrecht in 1965. He subsequently became Professor of Old Testament at the Catholic Theological High School in Amsterdam in 1969, at the Catholic University of Nijmegen in 1984 and the Catholic University of Louvain in 1989. He has been visiting professor at Mundelein Seminary, Chicago; the Jesuit School of Theology, Berkeley; and the University of Pretoria. He is also a member of the advisory board for the *Journal for the Study of the Old Testament*. He has published a four-part commentary on Isaiah 40–66 (1979–1990) and other Old Testament studies, above all on the books of Isaiah and Psalms.

Address: Waversebaan 220, B–3001 Leuven-Heverlee, Belgium

RICHARD HORSLEY is professor in the Classics and Religion Department, University of Massachusetts, Boston. He has written numerous articles on I Corinthians and popular Jewish movements at the time of Jesus; recent books are: *Bandits, Prophets, and Messiahs* (with John S. Hanson), San Francisco 1985; *Jesus and the Spiral of Violence: Popular Jewish Resistance in Roman Palestine*, San Francisco 1987, reissued Minneapolis 1992; *The Liberation of Christmas: The Infancy Narratives in Social Context*, New York 1989; *Sociology and the Jesus Movement*, New York 1989.

Address: Classics and Religion Department, University of Massachusetts, Harbor Campus, Boston, Mass., USA.

SEÁN FREYNE is currently Professor of Theology at Trinity College, Dublin, having previously lectured in biblical studies in the USA and Australia. He studied theology at the Pontifical University of Maynooth, Ireland, followed by specialized biblical studies in Rome, Jerusalem and the *Institutum Judaicum* of the University of Tübingen. He is the author of a number of books and articles in the areas of Early Christianity and Second Temple Judaism, most recently *Galilee, Jesus and the Gospels. Literary Approaches and Historical Investigations*, Dublin 1988. He joined the editorial board of *Concilium* in 1987.

Address: 24 Charleville Road, Dublin 6, Ireland.

JACOB NEUSNER was born in the United States in 1928 and studied at Harvard, the Jewish Theological Seminary of America and Columbia University, before going on to Lincoln College, Oxford, for further research. From 1968 he was Professor of Religious Studies at Brown University, and is now Graduate Research Professor of Humanities and Religious Studies at the University of South Florida, Tampa. He is the distinguished author of a wealth of books on Judaism and has made a new translation of the Mishnah.

MARCEL POORTHUIS was born in Hilversum in 1955 and studied theology at the Catholic University of Utrecht, where he graduated in Judaica; in 1983 he completed music studies at the Hilversum Conservatory. Since then he has been half-time study secretary of the Catholic Council for Israel. He also works at the Folkertsma Foundation for Talmudic Studies in Hilversum, where he is working on a thesis about the Talmudic commentaries of the Jewish philosopher Levinas. He has written *Abinou, Onze Vader*, Utrecht 1986 (with T. de Kruijf); *De joodse groeperingen ten tijde van Jezus*, Den Bosch 1989; and *Hamer op de rots: Over teksten en hun uitleg in jodendom en christendom*, Hilversum 1989.

Address: Katholieke Raad voor Israel, Biltstraat 121, 3572 APO Utrecht, Netherlands.

MARCUS VAN LOOPIK was born in 1950; he is a specialist in Jewish studies and gained his doctorate at the Free University of Amsterdam in 1992 with a thesis on messianism in Jewish literature, *Het Messiaanse Perspective van de Synagogale Liturgische Cyclus*. In addition to a number of articles on Jewish topics he has written *De Tien Woorden in de Mekhilta*, Sleutelteksten IV, Delft 1987, and *The Ways of the Sages and the Way of the World*, Texte und Studien zum Antiken Judentum 26, Tübingen 1991.

Address: Reaumurlaan 12, 1222 LT Hilversum, Netherlands.

HELGA ROBINSON-HAMMERSTEIN is Senior Lecturer in Modern History and Dean of Graduate Studies in Trinity College, Dublin. She gained her PhD from Marburg and researches into the transmission of ideas in the Reformation period. She is assistant pastor in the Lutheran Church in Dublin.

Address: University of Dublin, Trinity College, Dublin 2, Ireland.

ALISTAIR KEE was born in Scotland and studied economics and theology at Glasgow University. After gaining his MA and PhD at Union Theological Seminary, New York, he taught in the University College of Rhodesia (now Zimbabwe) before moving to the University of Hull, England. He then taught at the University of Glasgow and is now Professor of Religious Studies and Head of the Department of Theology and Religious Studies in the University of Edinburgh. His publications include *Constantine versus Christ* (1982), *Domination or Liberation* (1986) and *Marx and the Failure of Liberation Theology* (1990).

Address: Faculty of Divinity, University of Edinburgh, Edinburgh, Scotland.

JON SOBRINO was born in the Basque country in 1938. He joined the Society of Jesus in 1956 and has been a member of the Jesuit province of Central America since 1957. Ordained priest in 1969, he holds a degree in Philosophy and Letters as well as a Master's in engineering from St Louis University and a doctorate in theology from Frankfurt. His publications translated into English include *Christology at the Crossroads* (8th printing, 1984), *The True Church and the Poor* (1984), *Jesus in Latin America* (1986) and *Spirituality of Liberation* (1988). He is at present working on volume two of a new christology, of which volume one is scheduled for publication in English in 1993.

ROSEMARY RADFORD RUETHER is the Georgia Harkness Professor of Applied Theology at the Garrett-Evangelical Theological Seminary in Evanston, Illinois, and is the author or editor of twenty-three books on theology and social justice.

Address: Garrett-Evangelical Theological Seminary, 2121 Sheridan Road, Evanston, I11 60201, USA.

Members of the Advisory Committee for Exegesis

Directors

Wim Beuken SJ	Heverlee-Louvain	Belgium
Seán Freyne	Dublin	Ireland

Members

Luis Alonso Schökel SJ	Rome	Italy
John Ashton	Oxford	Great Britain
Hans Barstad	Oslo	Norway
Germain Bienaimé	Tournai	Belgium
Brendan Byrne SJ	Parkville/Vict.	Australia
Antony Campbell SJ	Parkville/Vict.	Australia
J. Cheryl Exum	Chestnut Hill/Ma.	USA
Aelead Cody OSB	St Meinrad/Ind.	USA
Vicente Collado Bertomeu	Valencia	Spain
José Severino Croatto CM	Buenos Aires	Argentina
Lucas Grollenberg OP	Nijmegen	The Netherlands
Herbert Haag	Lucerne	Switzerland
Bas van Iersel SMM	Nijmegen	The Netherlands
Hans-Winfried Jüngling SJ	Frankfurt/Main	Germany
Othmar Keel	Freiburg	Switzerland
Hans-Josef Klauck	Würzburg	Germany
Jonathan Magonet	London	Great Britain
Sean McEvenue	Montreal/Quebec	Canada
Martin McNamara MSC	Blackrock/Co. Dublin	Ireland
Halvor Moxnes	Oslo	Norway
Roland Murphy O Carm	Washington, DC	USA
Robert Murray SJ	London	Great Britain
Magnus Ottosson	Uppsala	Sweden
John Riches	Glasgow	Great Britain
Elisabeth Schüssler Fiorenza	Cambridge/Ma.	USA
Angelo Tosato	Rome	Italy
Marc Vervenne	Louvain	Belgium
Adela Yarbro Collins	Notre Dame/Ind.	USA

Members of the Advisory Committee for Church History

Director

Anton Weiler   Heelsum   The Netherlands

Members

Giuseppe Alberigo	Bologna	Italy
Roger Aubert	Louvain-la-Neuve	Belgium
Matthew Black	St Andrews	Scotland
Johannes Bornewasser	H. Landstichting	Netherlands
Victor Conzemius	Lucerne	Switzerland
Enrique Dussel	Mexico City	Mexico
John Tracy Ellis	Washington, DC	USA
J. Kloczowki	Lublin	Poland
Jan van Laarhoven	Nijmegen	The Netherlands
Giacomo Martina SJ	Rome	Italy
Heiko Oberman	Tucson, AZ	USA
Bernard Plongeron	Paris	France
Emile Poulat	Paris	France
Paolo Sinicalco	Rome	Italy
José Tellechea	San Sebastian	Spain
Brian Tierney	Ithaca, NY	USA